The Log of a Forty-Niner

Also from Westphalia Press

westphaliapress.org

The Log of a Forty-Niner

by Carolyn Hale Russ

WESTPHALIA PRESS
An imprint of Policy Studies Organization

The Log of a Forty-Niner
All Rights Reserved © 2014 by Policy Studies Organization

Westphalia Press
An imprint of Policy Studies Organization
1527 New Hampshire Ave., NW
Washington, D.C. 20036
info@ipsonet.org

ISBN-13: 978-1-63391-093-5
ISBN-10: 1633910938

Cover design by Taillefer Long at Illuminated Stories:
www.illuminatedstories.com

Daniel Gutierrez-Sandoval, Executive Director
PSO and Westphalia Press

Rahima Schwenkbeck, Director of Media and Marketing
PSO and Westphalia Press

Updated material and comments on this edition
can be found at the Westphalia Press website:
www.westphaliapress.org

The Log of a Forty-Niner

BEING THE RECORD OF AD-
VENTURES BY SEA AND
SHORE TO THE CALIFORNIA
GOLD-FIELDS AND THE PA-
CIFIC NORTHWEST, 1849–1854.

ILLUSTRATED FROM ORIGI-
NAL SKETCHES BY THE
AUTHOR.

EDITED FROM ORIGINAL
MANUSCRIPTS; NOW FOR
THE FIRST TIME PUBLISHED.

(*From an old Daguerreotype*)

Richard L. Hale

THE LOG OF A FORTY-NINER

Journal of a Voyage from Newbury-port to San Francisco on the Brig Gen'l Worth Commanded by Capt. Samuel Walton

Kept by

Richard L. Hale Newbury Mass.

CAROLYN HALE RUSS

B. J. BRIMMER COMPANY
BOSTON, MASS.
1923

FOREWORD

TRUE incidents chronicled by an author of his personal experiences, wherein he enacts the role of hero or victim are always, I think, filled with lively interest to the reader. When such circumstances are closely woven into the woof of a country's early memorials, — when the course of time in its progress leaves certain out-standing tracings, like distinct figures slowly threaded upon a beautiful and symmetrical tapestry, then these tracings become history.

Within the pages of this book are held the records of many events and thrilling adventures, in which my father was the chief actor, during the years of 1849 to 1854, both in California and the — at that time — great unexplored northwest.

The notes comprising the journal were given into my keeping ten years ago. As they then had slumbered for more than half a century, so likewise with me had they remained asleep! until an hour should come, and now is, when they were to go forth as records of those early days in a primitive land.

My father was of the family of Hales who came to New England from old England in pioneer days. Of the three brothers to leave the mother country in 1635 his ancestor settled in Newbury. From that sturdy stock came Nathan Hale, the "martyr spy," and back in England Sir Mathew Hale, famed as the only judge judging righteous judgment in an unrighteous time. My father was married in 1857 to Hannah Sewell Perley of Ipswich, a descendant of Allen Perley who sailed for America in Gov. Winthrop's fleet.

In my childhood I had listened to these stories of adventure as many another child has listened to fairy tales. The magical isle of Juan Fernandez became to my young mind a commingling of fact and fancy — a dream island whereon my father and Robinson Crusoe had been exiled together. The boy who had left home and gone so far, far away in search of the golden fleece, which he was never to find, was the subject for many a bed-time story, and the giant trees of Oregon, reaching up into the clouds, became a fairyland forest, — a wood of enchantment.

The facts as related in the journal have been carefully retained, and the course of events has not been disturbed; only where a break in the thread of the narrative has occurred have I tried to supply the intervening happenings as told to me on some evening perhaps, when in a mood for reminiscence, my father lived over his early manhood days in young San Francisco, or in the wild, unsettled northwest.

CAROLYN HALE RUSS.

CONTENTS

LIST OF ILLUSTRATIONS

*Nearly all the illustrations in "The Log of a Forty-Niner"
are made from pencil drawings by the author, Richard Lunt
Hale, in his journal kept during his trip to and from the gold
fields of California in 1849 to 1854. These pencil drawings
were carefully traced in ink by artists and were then repro-
duced by the photo-engraving process.*

HANNAH PERLEY HALE
WIFE OF RICHARD LUNT HALE

(From an old Daguerreotype)

TO
MY MOTHER
IN LOVING AND GRATEFUL
MEMORY.

PHOTOGRAPHIC REPRODUCTION OF THE FIRST PAGE OF
RICHARD HALE'S JOURNAL

The Log of a Forty-Niner

Brig General Worth Running Down S. E. Trades,
Pacific Ocean, 1850

Chapter I

FULL-RIGGED AND AWAY

NEWBURYPORT, Wednesday, November 28, 1849. To-day all hands mustered on board the little brig *General Worth* of Newburyport, Capt. Samuel Walton commanding. After bidding our friends a hearty good-by, which was responded to with ringing cheers, and moistened eyes by those left behind, the brig spread its wings, and flew down the harbor before a strong northwest breeze. At eleven-thirty A. M., being outside the bar — discharged our pilot, and laid our course southeast.

Thursday, 29th. We are now making good headway to south east. By our first observation at 12 M., the brig is in Latitude 41° 45′ north, Longitude 68° 14′ west. At 1 P. M. Halibut Point bears south-west, and from here we take our departure. Good-by dear old friends, and dear old Newburyport too! We watch the last lingering view until it sinks behind the wave. I almost regret the step I have taken. God grant we may meet again! The *General Worth* is now well out to sea — the wind still strong and favoring — the ocean rough. Many of the passengers are seasick, including myself, — some too sick to eat, others picking, — a few trying to make the best of it, but their looks speak more plainly than words. We all need "sea legs" at present, — rations are easy.

Saturday, December 1st. Wind still strong, and growing stronger. Our first accident occurred this afternoon in carrying away the topmast studding sail boom, which was soon replaced by a new one. Took in main royal, fore-top-gallant sail and mainsail. The wind lessening, soon set them again, with the topmast studding sail. The breeze still continues fine and fair, and at noon we find ourselves in Latitude 38° 22′ N., Longitude 62° 12′ W. Still steering southeast.

Sunday, December 2nd. The wind growing so much stronger, we double reefed fore, and single reefed main topsails. This evening passed through large schools of flying-fish. One of them attracted by our lights, and perhaps more curious than his fellows, paid us a visit. All had a look at him, then gave him his liberty.

Monday, December 3rd. Somewhat cloudy, with a fine breeze. Shook out reefs, and set light sails. A large ship in sight, also a brig steering west. Passed thousands of "Spanish-men-of-war," with all sails set on their tiny craft. Fine little navigators, these! But where they take their pugnacious name from is certainly a conundrum to me. They seem a peaceful set of little fellows, without guns, ammunition or warlike spirit. Each managing his own molluscan bark with the skill or the instinctive gifts, as it may be, far ahead of some of our larger deep sea pilots. By observation today we are in Latitude 35° 18′ N., Longitude 56° 34′ W.

Thursday, December 6th. Fine, pleasant weather. Breeze still fair. The passengers, most of them, having settled their accounts with Father Neptune are fast getting into shape again. It is really amusing to see some of them taking their little strolls about the deck, bent like half opened jackknives; about as graceful as schoolboys on stilts, grasping at whatever may help them keep their balance. Even the best of them are sadly in need of "sea legs." A few have ventured several ratlines up the rigging; one even so far as the futtock shrouds. But his courage failed him here, and with trembling hands, and careful feet, he beat a retreat as fast as his uncertain members would allow him, not giving even the "lubber hole" consideration. Some are playing cards, others reading, but on the whole all are a very grave, sedate and peace-loving set of fellows — at present. The crew are mending sails, and making mats for ship use.

Thursday, December 13th. Calm and warm. Yesterday and today are the warmest since leaving home. The vessel making not much headway, and the ocean being so smooth and tempting, many of us plunged overboard for a swim, taking the opportunity when our female shipmate was below. It really seemed as though we were at home again, diving from father's wharf into the Merrimac — splashing water at each other, diving, ducking, until warned by the captain to come on board, as he could see a breeze rippling the surface of the sea in the distance. His orders were right, for we were soon running under a strong wind, though not fair, still preferable to a monotonous calm. Beside our swimming we have passed the time in reading, writing, wrestling, singing, et cetera. The crew unbending old fair weather sails, and bending on new ones, getting into shape for rougher weather. Today spoke the brig *Samuel* of Beaufort, South Carolina, twenty-four days from Baltimore for San Francisco. Latitude 23° 45′ north, Longitude 35° 04′ west.

Friday, December 14th. Strong southerly wind. Ran through schools of flying-fish. At 8 A. M. a large brig passed us, steering N. N. W. Signaled but received no answer. Captain said "A Spanish hog!" Today we are 2,140 miles from Newburyport.

Saturday, December 15th. Light south and easterly winds. A brig passed us steering north. For the past three or four days we have had light and head winds. We have vainly prayed or whistled for a change — something, anything to break the tedious monotony. Every sailor well knows what this means, for it is confined to the ocean, and has not yet reached the shore. Light head winds and calms! Rolling! Slatting! Seasaw! Grinding! — water motion only; — not wind enough to steer or steady the old, lazy craft; — its only use, a sort of life-preserver — a cage for the blues! — the rails our fence, the deck our only pavement, — same old faces — same old voices; two suns by day, the reflected one in the glassy mirror of the sea more disagreeable than the one blazing down from the zenith. This has been a prolonged calm in the tropics. A little wind, even a head wind would be better. This afternoon had the good luck to capture two dolphins on a trail line. Notwithstanding our interest as we watched the changing colors of the dying beauties, we all enjoyed a dainty supper of fried dolphin. It was a delicious variation to our regular bill of ship diet. Today crossed the Tropic of Cancer in Longitude 34° 44′ west.

Friday, December 21st. So little of interest has occurred since the last record to break the monotony of sea life, the interval is passed over as unworthy of notice. An occasional sail breaks the horizon, or some wandering seabird wings past us. The bravest of us have taken trips aloft, for we are fast getting into sea trim. Some of us have even braved the danger of crossing the futtock shrouds. A few have laid out on the yardarm, while fewer still have touched the trucks or sat astride the jib boom end. If the light airs or calms hold on, we shall all be "fair weather sailors" soon.

Today noticed a fine red sand covering every available spot from truck to chain plate; spars, sails, rigging, deck all clothed in a light, beautiful coat of red, as evenly laid on as though a careful hand had dusted it there. The captain tells us it came from the African coast; borne aloft into clouds by the desert sand-storms, wafted sea ward by the offshore winds, and freighted by the dampness of the night air, it fell, a soft red dust, upon our brig. It seemed a little fictitious at first, as the African coast is at least five hundred miles distant.

Chapter II

THE ARENA ON THE SPAR DECK

Now I have had opportunity and time to become acquainted with the *General Worth's* passengers, and her crew. Captain Walton, our commander, has proved himself to be a thorough seaman, but also a strict disciplinarian. His rule is absolute, and he will brook no dictation, nor suggestion. If he is not obeyed, and that promptly, a volley of strong language bombards the offender. But he is a careful and conscientious captain in whom all have unbounded confidence.

The first and second mates are good seamen, and understand and do their duty. On the whole, the ship's royal family is all that could be desired.

DAVID PINGREE, COOK

The cook, David Pingree by name, is many men in one, — very original — it is kinder so to call him than eccentric — one of his kind! He seems as rugged as the granite of his native state, the unyielding hills of New Hampshire. He is a fine cook at his post in the galley, and there is no better, nor more willing sailor among the crew, — always good natured, and jovial, and a general favorite. When on duty he wears a blue flannel shirt and over-alls, with bare feet and bare head. The call will come to make or shorten sail. David springs out — the first to respond. Up into the rigging he climbs, just as he left his pots in the galley — lays out to the yard's end, or passes the earing, as nimble as a squirrel, seemingly as tough as the rigging he so lightly ascends. I have seen him after an hour's work aloft, still in bare feet and over-alls, while a freezing storm was raging, come down the rigging joking, and laughing at the fellows in thick flannels, and pea-jackets, with their heavy boots, —"storm clads" he calls them — give the sailors warning against carrying so much ballast aloft.

"If I fall, I can swim and be saved. You would be a gone case! You could no more float than the windlass bit, or the anchor."

Unlike many in the galley, he never "growls." Everything with David is always all right, and a broad smile usually illumines his weather-beaten face. We all like David, and what is hardly to be expected, like his cooking as well as his seamanship.

JAMES GUTTERSON

James Gutterson from Nova Scotia, is David's opposite. Jimmy, we call him, is working his passage as one of the crew, but he never, never will become a good sailor; — good hearted, well-intentioned, very willing when his duty permits him to remain on deck, but aloft, wholly out of his element. He never yet has reached the top, and never will. He starts up the rigging with the others, but gets no higher than a few ratlines, — there grasping the shrouds with a death-like grip, and setting his knees against the ratlines above, he cautiously ascends, keeping his right foot ahead, and his eyes glued to the deck.

After the crew have finished, and are on their way down again, they pass him there like a fixed object — a portion of the rigging, apparently immovable, and so he is, for he does not dare loosen his grip or attempt to change his position until the spot to which he so closely clings is absolutely still.

Sailors must have their little jokes, often at the expense of their shipmates, and poor Jimmy often comes in for some of their pranks. On shipboard there is small sympathy for the sailor who is afraid.

Some of the old wags, in descending the rigging, while near him would give it a tremendous shake, then hasten to apologize for their blunder. But, Jimmy only hugged the closer, doubtless not caring much, in his dread position, whether it was done intentionally or not. Once when all was calm, he touched the futtock-shrouds, but usually neither threats nor persuasion can induce him to go aloft. As a sailor Jimmy is a complete failure.

Surely, many types of men are gathered together within the decks of this small brig. With a common cause to weld them, their very eccentricities help to pass the slow-moving hours more agreeably.

JOE

Joe has a most amusing idea of the capacity of a brig's storage — for his own personal dainties. Everyone calls him Joe. Without doubt he boasts another appellative, but if he does, I have not heard it. There are always two estimates of a man — his shore and sea rating. From Joe's appearance, when at last he raised up from his

Farewell to the Brig General Worth.

Away gallant Brig amid foam and in spray,
O'er ocean's dark billows; oh speed thee away;
Stout hearts are on board of true puritan stock,
Who reck not of tempest, who danger will mock,
And they tread with the step of the bold and the free;
Our prayers shall go with them far over the sea.

Away gallant brig, where the fresh breezes blow,
Course on through the trades with thy pinions of snow;
The shark and the dolphin will mark thy career,
And the whale gambol round thee un short or in fear;
Where the Cross of the South lights ye on as ye roam,
Shall the sons of the Merrimack think of their home?

Speed on gallant vessel, and cross ye the Line,
Old Neptune will hail from his palace of brine;
But a name is your passport, he'll trouble you not,
And cheers will ascend from Amphytrite's court;
'Tis only a coaster, the Triton will sing,
As away on your track like a racer ye spring.

And when off Cape Horn, as ye scud in a gale,
With every thing snug under closely reefed sails,
Where the albatross skims in her slow circling flight,
And left far behind are the regions of night,
While the boys tell long yarns of the girls that they love,
May their bosoms be true and their trust be above.

Ye shall coast the fair shore that the standard enslaved,
Where gold was the prize for the danger he braved;
Ye shall pass the green Isles where the savages dwell,
Where the cocoanut grows amid coral and shell,
Till the pine-covered banks, where your lot may have cast,
And the flower painted meadows, shall greet ye at last.

Then away gallant vessel, in foam and in spray,
Over ocean's blue billows speed bounding away,
May the brave hearts who leave us of Puritan stock,
Stand firm in temptation as old Plymouth Rock;
May they tread in the steps of the bold and the free,
And our prayers shall go with them far over the sea.

agony of seasickness, one would say, that he probably passed for a man of considerable *standing* when on terra firma, but this cape voyage has damaged his reputation. When he shipped, the quantity of his baggage caused much comment among passengers and crew, and it was soon noised about that fresh, delicious eatables were stowed away within those bulky parcels.

For weeks Joe lay so wretchedly sick that no dainty however tempting, could draw him from his berth. At length, the fine tropical weather, with smooth, calm seas, gave him fresh courage and revived his hunger. His thoughts immediately turned to the pies, nuts and candy, pickles and preserves, and also the firkin of tripe, so carefully secreted in a little room beneath the pantry. In this direction Joe hastened with keen anticipation, but with surreptitious footsteps. These toothsome delicacies belonged to him, and were to be shared with no one else. To his great chagrin and disappointment, the concealed corner was absolutely bare! Everything had disappeared! — not a vestige remained of his treasures! The reason for the mysterious disappearance was this: during Joe's long illness, the mate had taken a survey of that very nook in which was hidden the valuable collection of fresh groceries. A disagreeable odor led the keen nose of the watchful mate to this secluded spot, and here he found to his great indignation, the decayed and rancid store of food Joe had concealed. In less time than it takes to write the unfortunate sequel to the story of Joe's larder, the things appeared on deck. Those that were still edible found their way into the eager mouths of the boys who were fortunate enough to get them, while the larger amount sank into the briny sea. Thus ended the story of "Joe's dainties."

It is impossible to appreciate the value of fresh food on shipboard. The usual fare is hard baked biscuit, called by the sailors "hard-tack," baked very hard to prevent moulding, and beef as salt as salt itself, to keep it from spoiling, named in sea-language "salt-junk," and "salt-horse" with "duff" or boiled pudding, served once a week, and a hash when they are fortunate enough to have potatoes, while an occasional dish of beans, together with tea and coffee constitute the sea-going bill of fare.

The continued use of salt food often causes attacks of scurvey, then the only remedy lies in fresh vegetables, to be had by a forced stop at some harbor along the way. It may have been that Joe bore this fact in mind when he shipped his supply, but however well his intentions, the result proved anything but happy. Yet, Joe showed himself to be considerably of the nature of a stoic. His face betrayed no emotion when the laughing shipmates clustered around him. In fact, no matter what the occasion, he never indulged in mirth nor passion — rarely smiled, never joked, minded his own business, and courted no favors. He came from the farming lands of Massachusetts, and, I think, owned much property there. Joe was headed for the gold-fields like the rest of us.

A company of forty-five members, dependent upon their own resources of temperaments and personalities to while away months of loneliness, within the limitations of a small vessel, must necessarily find some outlet for amusement; at least, the fact remains, whether it is to be deplored or not, that some one among that company, sooner or later, becomes the butt of the wags, while the others look on and apparently enjoy the fun. There was a little fellow on board named Mose. He melted to flattery as butter to heat; he hungered for it, and would perform any sort of ridiculous feat if he were but praised. And yet this undersized man possessed the brain of a born trader, for no barter ever found Mose on the losing side, — the balance ever fell to his credit. But his weakness for flattery was soon discovered, and then the boys set about to bespatter him with it. He accepted this all in good faith, finally believing himself to be the most important man on the brig, not excepting the captain. He swelled larger and larger, until he imagined that he could whip any man on shipboard. Like the fabled frog, he grew more and more inflated, but his hour for bursting had been carefully prepared by his seemingly innocent comrades.

Among the passengers was a big fellow, nicknamed "Nuck." He frequently wrestled with Mose, and always went down before him. These successive triumphs (?) brought unlimited praise for the diminutive hero (?) who now fancied himself to be the most powerful man aboard. A committee of three was formed, with J. Titcomb of Newburyport, as chairman. He had a keen sense of humor, and was one of the brightest and most capable amongst us.

It had been decided to have three exhibitions of valor, with "Nuck" and Mose as the chief actors. The arena opened upon the spar deck, just in front of the forward house, and the matches always occurred during the captain's afternoon naps. This place was completely concealed from the view of the after cabin. The opening number consisted of a round between Mose and "Nuck." "Nuck" made his entrance, with most impressive manner, bared to the waist. He was a head taller than the fiery little "champion," with splendidly developed muscles, and at least sixty pounds heavier. He could easily have picked up his small opponent and thrown him over the rail.

The day, calm and lovely, offered a most favorable time for the exciting event. We gathered in our places, leaving an opening in the center through which the gladiators should make their entrance. In the midst of much hand clapping came Mose in full ring attire, with confident swagger, strutting under the very nose of his opponent.

It was to be the best in three. After a half-hour of severe wrestling "Nuck" went down amid much hissing, and wild huzzas for Mose. This moment was the proudest of the little fellow's life, and he fully believed himself capable to vanquish anyone who should stand before him. Then came much sponging off, and rubbing down, followed by the second bout. "Nuck" came to the ring crestfallen, and with hanging head, while the victorious Mose proudly entered, bravely wearing his honours in all good faith. The boys had crowded around him; had shaken his hand as though it were a very great privilege; had patted him on the back and proclaimed him a wonderful fighter, and he had swallowed it all as a very pleasant sugar-plum.

In the second round "Nuck" again went down. This was followed by still more shouts for "Mose the champion" — while his huge adversary received only hisses and execrations. The third and last battle arrived, with the result that here again Mose scored an overwhelming conquest. This settled it! Mose was the acknowledged champion of the vessel! He was crowned the victor, while "Nuck" slunk away, followed by the hisses of the crowd.

The following week another exhibition took place, the weather favoring as before, the captain and second officer sleeping below, while the mate, who was the officer of the deck, apparently knew nothing of what was going on. "Nuck" now perhaps, might redeem himself. An hour of terrific (?) struggle followed, but in the end, down went "Nuck"! — little Mose had thrown the big fellow again. Now, the champion sent his challenge to anyone on board ship to meet and wrestle with him. But no one seemingly had sufficient courage. A feat of vaulting followed, with little Mose out-jumping all contestants; and so on, with other athletic features — running, handsprings, et cetera. In each sport he carried off the palm. At the conclusion of these many victories, the small hero completely ruled the ship, holding a court as undisputed as any monarch on his throne. Each one passed him with a deep salaam, which he very kindly acknowledged by a condescending dip of his head.

But, alas, his hour was approaching. The frog had almost distended to his utmost capacity!

The final hour of contests drew near, and as ever, the

day selected, dawned bright and calm, for only under fair and sunny skies, with placid seas, could the exhibitions occur.

The first number proved to be a vaulting test over a capstan bar, one end of which rested on the rail, while the other was held by the "manager." Mose ran and leaped into the air! just at that moment the bar flew up, and Mose's toes went under, while his whole body sprawled upon the deck in a most (to him) unexpected manner. He did not observe the trick, but rose rather shame-facedly, and entered all the more heartily into the next competition, which centered upon the runners. The entries lined up, and at the word were off, but, somehow, Mose instead of coming in first, laid flat upon the deck. A mysterious rope had arisen in front of his flying feet, and had thrown him face downward among the runners. How-ever, in this inglorious attitude, his hand touched the goal, he claimed the victory, and the manager allowed it.

Now, came the final wrestling match. Mose of course, being champion, entered the ring in fine feather, wholly confident, his chest inflated, and his every move breathing defiance and menace to his opponent. The next smallest man on the brig had been selected to wrestle with him, and at once, he put Mose flat upon his back. As though suddenly dawning upon his befuddled brain that he had been made a laughing stock, Mose gathered himself together, shook his head, that only yesterday had nodded with such condescension, and mopping his brow said,

"This is enough! No more fooling for Mose!"

It was these little diversions in the dull routine of ship life, that made the long hours within the brig pass more quickly; and while, perhaps, the amusement might have savoured of a kindlier nature, it yet was innocent enough, with no malice to injure the object of the fun.

JAMES A. VARNEY

One other of the after cabin family I must mention — James A. Varney. In his home in Maine he had taught music. Many a calm evening, underneath the stars, here on shipboard, he has entertained us, both with his violin — he is a fine violinist — and by the clear tones of his voice. It has been most enjoyable to have this talented man among us. He has been generous of his gifts, adding the sweet sounds of *his* music to the rippling music of the water falling back from the bow of the brig, while we passengers gathered round to listen to his violin, or to hear the songs of the hour, with occasionally a solo from an opera ringing out over the ocean.

He has left an undying sign upon some of our arms, for he is an artist at tattooing. On mine there is an olive wreath, with a dove and an eagle — a never fading keepsake, it will go with me to my grave! *

We are fast becoming a united family. It is easily seen that our common interests are causing us to become necessary to one another, and when the time comes to disband, it will be with many regrets that we are forced to separate; but, as widely differing as are our temperaments and vocations, there is ever the one motive driving us forward — gold!

---

* Upon the arm of the author, many years after, in blue ink, with an occasional touch of red, curved the delicate wreath so early transferred there by Mr. Varney.

Chapter III

AN UNINTENTIONAL INSULT

T HURSDAY, December 27th. Light baffling winds and showery. Yesterday left the trades, or rather they left us. Our voyage has not been highly favoured by the northeast trades. We did not take them until reaching Latitude 20° N. Often they are felt several degrees farther north. Now, for the Doldrums — light, baffling, changeable winds, or calms — more grumbling in the outlook. All who read can see that we are fast becoming seasoned sailors, for the "old salt," as he is called, claims the right to "growl" at something; the bad smelling "salt-junk," "old monkey," "hard-tack," tough, rubbery "duff," the scanty measure of weak coffee, or the unsweetened drug, called tea. If not these, his messmate must suffer. But, first of all we are a band of anxious gold-seekers, — all bent on making our fortunes. And we want to get about it quickly. All delays cause more unrest than anything else.

Today caught a young shark. He was not allowed to die a natural death — this wolf of the ocean. He was given to his native elements again, there undoubtedly, to be received with open mouths, by those he would have devoured. Two little visitors made us a call this morning, and are still with us swimming in the eddy waters caused by the motion of the rudder, — two little pilot fish, and

ISLAND OF FERNANDO NOVONHU, COAST OF SOUTH AMERICA.

two little welcome beauties they are! — about the size of small mackerel, girt with dark rings.

One thing worthy of note, and which I neglected to record was speaking of our first ship, since leaving Newburyport. It was on the 24th of this month: *The Hamden* of Boston, twenty-seven days from New York. When first sighted, she was steering a south, southeast course. We continued to shorten the distance between us until within four miles, when she set a signal for speaking, which we answered, and hove to. She ran down, and while passing us threw a bundle of letters on board for us to take to St. Catharine's, as they were to make no stop on the voyage to San Francisco. They gave us three hearty cheers to which we as heartily responded, then we both proceeded on our course. Latitude 6° 44' N., Longitude 25° 14' W. Course south by west.

Monday, December 31st. Last Friday spoke the ship *Washington* of Petersburg, thirty-eight days from New York, bound for San Francisco. And yesterday the brig *William Tucker* of Bridport, England, thirty-five days from Liverpool for Buenos Aires, S. A. This is the last day of the year, and the last of our sailing in the northern Atlantic waters, for some time at least, for we crossed the Line in Longitude 29°, and are now laying our course southwest in the southern Atlantic. If Father Neptune hailed us, we did not hear him, and we sped on leaving him in his briny home, with his unused brush and pot As we were showing him our heels, the lines composed on our departure were repeated by many of us:

"Speed on gallant vessel and cross ye the Line,
Old Neptune will hail from his palace of brine,
But a name is your passport, he 'll trouble you not,
And cheers will ascend from Amphytrite's grot.
'T is only a coaster' the Tritons will sing,
As away on your course like a racer ye spring."

This is one verse of six, composed by a missionary friend, and given to us on leaving the wharf at Newburyport.

Wednesday, January 2, 1850. Second day of the new year. May it end with as much good cheer as it begins! We are having a strong southeast breeze, and laying our course southwest. Passed a ship far in the distance. With a glass we could discern her class, but she soon disappeared as she came — behind the horizon. At 10 A. M. saw the island of Fernando Novonhu bearing S. W. by W., the first land sighted since Cape Ann sank in our wake. Land, I say! Why it is a huge rock rising high above the sea. At a distance it resembles a cathedral with a lofty tower. It is in Latitude 3° 55' south, Longitude 22° 29', and about one hundred and ninety miles from the coast of Brazil. There has been some claim that this island was the scene of the exile of Alexander Selkirk — Robinson Crusoe — instead of Juan Fernandez in the Pacific, but I wholly discredit the idea. I believe it to be without foundation. It is a barren, forbidding looking, somber spot. The Captain tells us that Fernando Novonhu was used as a place of exile, and as a prison by the Brazilian government. Have put in time while passing in drawing sketches of the island.

Saturday, January 5th. Pleasant with a light southwest

wind. This afternoon passed through large schools of
cowfish, a warm-blooded, air-breathing animal, much resembling a porpoise, but considerably larger. The ocean
seemed alive with them. Thousands, perhaps tens of thousands sported as they passed, apparently wholly unconscious of the enemy within their midst. The captain with
his harpoon took a position on the bobstay, and secured
a fine, big fellow. We soon had him on deck and dressed
for the table. As he was hanging from the mainstay, he
looked like a great hog — a huge fellow, eight feet six
inches long, weighing at least four hundred pounds. His
flesh tasted much like beef, and was quite a luxury, for we
had been well salted down, and had long wished for a bite
of some fresh fish or bird, and he proved a good sea change.
The day ends as it began — pleasant with a light southeast breeze. Course still south, southwest, Latitude 10° 37'
south, Longitude 34° 35', west.

Wednesday, January 9th. Fine southeast breeze. We
are taking advantage of the gentle southeast trades which
we waylaid by taking an eastern stretch nearly across the
Atlantic. The baffling, uncertain northeast trades, as we
experienced them, died out some time before reaching the
equator, but the southeast trades soon taking their place
made our time in the doldrum latitudes of short duration.
This afternoon, we caught a young swordfish on the trail-
line. He was placed under the tender care of the cook,
who is really an expert in preparing fish for the table.
David is so skilful he could make a tempting bite of any
ocean captive, barring the shark, for this grizzly flesh

would serve better for footballs than food, even for not too critical sailors like ourselves.

Again in speaking of that dread foe of the ocean (the shark) there is but one handsome spot on his whole body, and that the most dreaded of all — his handsome terrible teeth. These creatures followed the brig, ready for a bite of anything fresh or salt, it mattered not to them — anything thrown from the boat found its way into their ravenous maws. They are a foe to everything that swims. Even one of their kind, if wounded, is soon devoured by his cannibalistic companions.

Tuesday, January 15th. Our fine southeast trades have left us, and in their place we are having bafflings, first strong, and then dwindling almost to a calm. Passed large red spots floating on the surface of the ocean, which our old sailors pronounced minute fish, often seen in these latitudes. For some days we have been getting things ready for port; changing sails, cleaning ship in and out board, painting, etc. Last week we passed two small boats steering south, which our deep water sailors call Portuguese fruiters. Also a barque and brigantine steering toward Rio Janeiro. We passed Cape Frio a little to the eastward of the craft, but did not sight it, the fog preventing. At 6 P. M. made the island of Santa Catharina bearing west, about twenty-five miles distant. At 8 P. M. we laid by for daylight. In the morning made sail and stood in toward the land, — shortly we entered the harbor, and anchored off the American Consul's house, where an officer boarded us, and ordered us to lay six days in quarantine. At anchor were two brigs, and a schooner; the *Quady Belle*, forty-eight days from Lubec, the *Maria*, sixty-three days from Bath, and the schooner *Emily Frances*, fifty-two days from Provincetown, — all for San Francisco. Not long afterward a steamer came into the harbor for a supply of coal, — receiving it, she left for sea with her fresh supply. Her place was soon filled by the whaling barque *Malta* of Tisbury, Martha's Vinyard, homeward bound from a two years' cruise on the whaling grounds of the Pacific. Thinking her not sea-worthy her captain put in here for repairs, which we all thought were sadly necessary. A more rusty looking set it would be hard to find, — a set of curios! Their clothes, old and oily, were not ragged, for they were ingeniously held together by sail-needle and twine, all making a complete whole of patch upon patch, covering the original garments so completely that it was hard to discriminate between first coat and repairs. But they were a lot of good, jolly fellows, mirthful, and fun loving, with healthy bodies and even handsome faces. By them we sent home letters.

St. Catharine's (Anglicized) presents a very lovely picture when viewed from the ocean or bay; its high, peaked rocks, its tree-covered mountains, always in living green from shore to summit, make a beautiful vista from the deck of the brig. The island is separated from the mainland by a narrow strait. The surrounding views of scattered isles dotting the blue waters, with nestling villages of shining white houses on the crescent shaped shores of its harbors, paint a scene long to be remembered — a paradis-

ian hiding place. There is a fine, safe harbor on the
south, and this makes one of the best stopping places for
vessels bound "round the Horn," for here there is water,
also provisions and fruit in abundance. This is my brother
Enoch's birthday; twenty-five years old today! I have
not forgotten it nor the dear good boy either. May he
live to see many, many more happy birthdays.

Wednesday, January 16th. This afternoon the American consul came alongside in a skiff rowed by four coloured
men. We learned from him that the barque *Domingo* and
the brig *Ark* from Newburyport left here just before we
arrived. The latter sailed from home about a month
before our departure. Today a party of fellows started in
one of our ship's boats for a trip round the harbor. We
took with us several boys from the schooner *Frances*
about as wild and as foolish as ourselves. We determined
to visit the old fort, and were within hailing distance,
when a sentinel warned us to stop. At the same time, he
commanded us not to land, with his musket levelled at
our crew, while a cannon was quickly wheeled to rake us
if so ordered. Not favouring such a warm reception we
quickly turned, and put the nose of the tender on the
offshore tack, but we gave them, while retreating, a lively
serenade of tunes, like Yankee Doodle, Hail Columbia,
etc. After finishing our lark, and returning our companions to their vessel, we leisurely steered toward our
own. But the reception our good old captain gave us as
the last man reached the deck, I never shall forget. Even
though severe, he was right. After eyeing us sternly, and

appearing to us more dangerous than the teeth of the old fort we had so ignorantly insulted, he said,

"You are a set of damned ignorant, insulting curs, who have escaped what you justly deserved, — being blown to hell by Spanish powder! — Trying to visit a foreign fort without the permit of its government, were you? — playing foreign national airs to aggravate the officers for honestly doing their duty, were you? — which by G—— they have neglected in sparing you."

Soon after the old capitan from the fort came on board — a nervous, irritable old hombre, quite small in stature, almost hidden in lace and epaulets, with a big, shaggy, white moustache covering his mouth that seemed to keep time to the constant twitching of his dark, angry face, and fierce glittering eyes. He addressed our captain, while we stood by, feeling anything but comfortable. He forbade boat-sailing, or landing for wood or water (a privilege granted by the quarantine office) until our quarantine was finished. Our captain at once explained the whole matter to him, not sparing us in the least, whereat the old Spaniard at once revoked the wood and water order. He seized our captain's hand, shaking it warmly, but he did not revoke his order against the *boat-sailing*. Then he gracefully turned toward Captain Walton, and with another hand-shake, and a glance at us that would have destroyed us if it had been a dagger, he took his departure.

The natives, brown, black, with a few whites, mostly a mixture of Spanish, Portuguese and negroes, in their little boats were our constant companions. They thronged the sides of the brig with all kinds of fruit for sale, they had learned enough from the vessels bound for California that have put in here, not to be cheated in trade, for they were not backward in putting high prices on their fruit, but would barter when their first offers were refused, or some other boat was ready to undersell them. They were indeed more cunning than shrewd, and though fierce looking, were considered harmless. The great object of these boat-venders seemed to be trade. Early each day boats of all sizes, freighted with the finest looking fruits were seen making for the inward bound vessels.

Monday, January 21st. Having laid out our quarantine, we got under way, and with a fair wind ran up the harbor, and anchored abreast the city of St. Catharine's. We are anticipating a great time tomorrow on shore! There we passengers have our liberty. Quite a treat, for we have been like caged birds! From our deck the little city looks very pleasant and inviting.

Tuesday, January 22nd. This morning made an early start for the city. Passed most of the day very pleasantly, visiting every place of note. It is a small town of some business. We counted three Catholic churches, a prison, and some good looking public buildings. Most of the houses are one-story adobies, with tiled roofs. The streets are narrow, crooked, and do not speak highly of the sanitary officers' attentions. This afternoon the crew are getting ready for a move down the harbor to finish wood and water supply — then another trip seaward. Were it

ISLAND OF FERNANDO NOVONIU

not for the great lookout ahead would like to remain here a few days longer. But the cry of "Gold!" "Gold!" is on the air, and every delay, however pleasant, makes us impatient.

Friday, January 25th. Last evening got under way and ran down to our old anchorage at Santa Cruz. At 2 P. M., having obtained everything necessary for another sea voyage, hoisted in our boats, weighed anchor, and put to sea again, with a strong southeast breeze. Soon skirting the headlands, we gave a last, lingering look to land, then turned our faces seaward. We are again on the boundless ocean, on our way to the gold-fields, and now the brig's company begin to realize that the most serious obstacles are before us. Those to be the most dreaded! That dangerous turning point Cape Horn must be weathered! Yet our fancy carries us safely past it, and in our dreams we often are on the homeward stretch heavily laden with the precious ore so much has been braved to discover.

Chapter IV

FIGHTING CAPE WEATHER

SUNDAY, February 10th. For the past fortnight but little has occurred worth recording. The same old sea monotony!—the sun rising from the water in the morning, and setting in it again at night, with an occasional sail in the distance. This is sea life in all its tiresome routine. Today we had the excitement of speaking our first vessel since leaving Santa Cruz. First the barque *Espeletta*, of Salem, Mass., seventy-eight days outward, bound for San Francisco. Soon afterwards spoke the brig *Reindeer* of Plymouth, Mass., sixty-nine days from New York, also bound for the gold-fields.

Today saw and caught our first albatros, on a trail line baited with pork. One eagerly snapped at it, and we quickly had him on board. Three others were caught with the same bait, making quite a flock. But they were shy, and avoided us, making a sort of "quacking" noise whenever we approached them. The birds did not seem to like our company, or their footing, for when they attempted to rise from the deck, they found it to be an impossibility. Only from the water can they gain their impetus. The largest measured ten feet ten inches from tip to tip of wings. Ornithology can boast of no more remarkable type than these wanderers of the ocean; having a body no larger than that of a goose, but with a vast spread of double-jointed wings that carry them gracefully in the teeth of the fiercest gale — turning, wheeling in their flight, apparently with the greatest ease, seeming to defy both wind and wave.

Our fine breeze has increased to a gale. We have taken in lighter sails, and close reefed topsails, making several tacks off and landward. At 6 A. M. set more sail and stood to east, with Staten Land about eight miles distant. It makes me shiver to look at this bleak, sterile pile of rock and snow, in Latitude 54° 47′, south, Longitude 63° 41′. Its surface is high, rugged and barren, topped by sharp, craggy peaks, covered with eternal snow. For thirty-six miles this uninhabited frozen wilderness lined the horizon. At 12 M. Cape St. John, its most eastern point bore west.

This is my eldest brother Charles' twenty-ninth birthday. A happy day to you, brother. May many more succeed it.

Friday, February 15th. During the past five days have had what is called "Cape Horn" weather. The dangerous turning point is now one hundred and eighty miles distant bearing north, northeast. We are experiencing every kind of weather, but calm and warm, — sudden squalls, gales, hail, sleet, rain, and often fierce squalls; coming without warning, and disappearing in the same mysterious way. Changing winds and changing waves are our constant companions, keeping the officers on the constant lookout, and the crew on the constant jump.

Sailing past Staten Land we kept it in sight from its eastern to its western boundary, and gladly bade good-by to the coast of rock and gloom, and to its ice-loving dwellers (ducks and penguins). Our course is, has been, and looks as though it might be for some time to come — full and by, that is, sailing as near the wind as possible. This is also called "close hauled." We are taking advantage of head winds the best we can. But our gain at present seems to be more north than south, while we impatiently wait for more favouring gales to waft us far from the detestable regions of sterile rocks, frozen skies, and cloudless squalls. No one can form a correct idea of these clear weather squalls without experiencing one of them. They come in veins or narrow currents, — without warning they are upon you!

A few days ago we were sailing in company with a brig. She was, perhaps, two miles to the windward of us. In an instant her flying jib was torn from its hanks, sheets, and halliards, and it was lost in the air, in less time than it takes to relate it, while all other parts of the vessel escaped injury. During the past few days we have passed several vessels, all like ourselves, trying to get farther south. Without doubt, they also are steering for the goldfields. One coming within hailing distance proved to be the brig *George Shaddock* of Boston, bound for San Francisco.

On February 22nd the entire brig's company observed a rousing celebration! Guns were fired, pistols, and everything noise-making brought from their hiding places. We did not forget to honour the father of his country on the anniversary of his natal day. Bonfires were *omitted*.

Friday, March 1st. Still here fighting Cape weather!
It is rougher than we thought it could be. Sleet, snow and
hail, the brig awash with raging brine much of the time!
Impossible to keep dry, or at all comfortable, with winds
varying and unsteady. Nothing certain, but the strong
current setting eastward. The crew are on the constant
jump — up rigging and down; shortening and making
sail, — the watch relieved hardly get below, before they
are called again for "all hands" duty. We sometimes hear
strong language — too strong to repeat. Vessels of various
grades and rigs have passed us near and far without
speaking. Among them we saw a small schooner coming
from the entrance of Magellan Strait, all undoubtedly
California bound.

Chapter V

ROBINSON CRUSOE LAND

At last we are on the broad Pacific, steering a north and west course, and, a thing greatly to be desired, the brig is just feeling the trades. This is my father's fifty-seventh birthday. My mother's occurred on September 20th. God bless them both. To-morrow March 2d will be my twenty-second birthday. I really feel much older. Perhaps this adventure has something to do with my sudden sensation of age.

Wednesday, March 6th. A fine, fair wind with pleasant weather. The crew engaged in bending on chains, and getting ready for port. Two things I have forgotten to mention, and very important ones in southern waters, are the Southern Cross, and the Magellan Clouds, which we first sighted in the doldrum latitudes. The Southern Cross is composed of four brilliant stars, forming the outer points of a cross. The Clouds are a golden mist upon the sky, of about the same density as our Milky Way. They are not only guides to the southern voyager, but companions to him in the long, weary watches of the night.

Thursday, March 7th. The *General Worth* is now five hundred miles north of the point where she first entered the Pacific, and fast gaining in her run up. All are happy at the thought the old Cape is far in our wake, and the "promised land," though not so near as we might wish, yet, it is not so very many hundred miles before us, with the greatest dangers of the journey over.

It would amuse some of the girls at home if they could take a bird's-eye view of our brig today. We are washing. It is a regular washing-day at sea. But there are no tubs or washing-boards, in their places we have clubs, mauling the wet, sopping clothes on the deck after they have been well towed on the trail line. Then with another severe clubbing, they are again towed until clean. The latter is the sailor's method of rinsing. After a long period of trailing over-board the clothing is hauled on deck and hung on lines stretched from all parts of the lower rigging. This is our plight today. Lines in all directions, filled with every grade and shade of garments! The girls would think, I fear, we look more like a laundry than a California droger. Washing-day with sailors is not every Monday as on shore, but when the clothing is too dirty to wear — when the spell comes on, and above all, when the weather is fitting. Then it goes through the whole ship like a contagion. Everybody has but one idea, and that is to maul, trail, and dry his clothing.

We are now getting into shape for port, — the most fascinating spot, to me, on the face of the globe! Robinson Crusoe's island! It is to be our next stopping-place. What schoolboy but is familiar with the name of Robinson Crusoe, and his man Friday? and what New England boy but has imagined himself a cast-away on this very island, watching and waving for the sail that does not appear, and finding untold pleasure in make-believe meals of roots and wild fruits. To-morrow I shall see the enchanted isle! Not the picture of fancy, but the real ground, the same trees, perhaps see the cave that Robinson dug, or the ruins of his little hovel, or some relic he may have left behind. The vision will become a reality. The very substance of the soil over which I may tread to-morrow will seem not more genuine to me than the pictures of my boyhood's fancy. They will live forever, as long as my mind has the power to act, or memory the power to recall.

Thursday, March 7th. Opens fair with a fine breeze from south. At 8.30 A. M. made the island of Juan Fernandez, about forty miles distant. At 2 P. M. dropped anchor in Cumberland Bay on its northeast side. Here at anchor lay the brig *Annah* of Newburyport, and I had the unexpected pleasure of seeing old friends from home. This afternoon all ashore enjoying our first land tramp since leaving St. Catharine's. It is really a lovely spot! — about ten miles in length, and less than half that extent in width, situated in Latitude 33° 40', south, Longitude 78° 56'. Its surface is very uneven, the side facing the bay gently rising from the shore to the base of its hills in natural sloping lawns. Behind the mountains are large, fertile valleys, where grow delicious fruits — pears, peaches, plums, figs, apricots, cherries, strawberries, and others, — all growing wild, in great abundance, with no one to harvest them. Juan Fernandez belongs to the government of Chili, and was formerly used as a place for

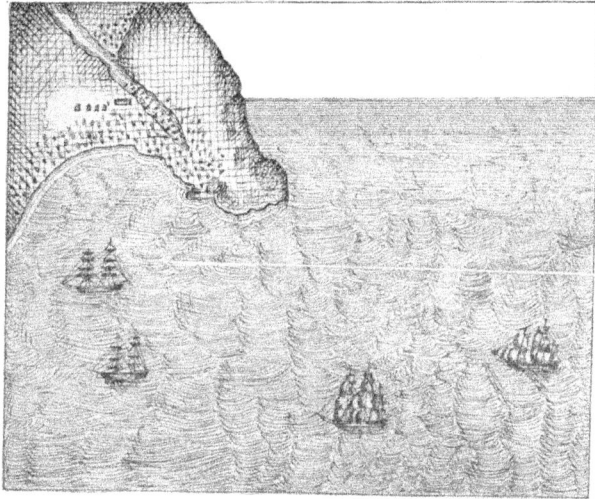

CUMBERLAND BAY, JUAN FERNANDEZ, 1850

convicts. The most hardened criminals were confined in caves on the mountain sides, and were strictly guarded by sentinels. Some of the caves, with the ruins of the old fort, are still to be seen, while the cannon now are used as posts for vessels to make fast to. It is said there is no better water to be had, or no better watering place on the islands of the Pacific than at Juan Fernandez. The water comes from mountain springs, and is brought to the shore by wooden conductors, that put out from the bank, just high and far enough to float a cask under for filling. There are but eleven inhabitants on the island, all native-born Chilians but one, and he is the harbor pilot — a smart-looking state of Maine man, with a Chilian wife. They occupy one of the cozy little cottages made of straw, with leaf-covered roofs, scattered along the hillside, overlooking the bay. These straw houses are the only style of architecture used by the inhabitants, and are really ingeniously made. A frame is first erected, then the straw woven closely up the sides until storm-proof. The roof caps the whole in the same, simple manner, but here large palm-leaves are so interwoven that they become water-proof. Each tiny house has one or two rooms, and from a distance these little homes look very picturesque and even inviting.

The woods of the island abound in game, and the harbor with fish. On the eastern side rise inaccessible, barren rocks, jagged and precipitous, warning all to land by some other route; chaos seems to reign, while just over the sharp crests of the mountains, beyond their desolate waste, lie the fertile valleys so tenderly protected by these grim sentries.

Friday, March 8th. Today is to be the day of great adventure! Not *the* great adventure, for that awaits us on the Pacific coast, at San Francisco. But it is to be a day from which I expect great things. I shall follow the footsteps of my hero, in imagination at least, and make a more thorough tour into the interior. I shall see sights that he saw, and perhaps, understand that feeling of loneliness that he felt on this deserted island. In this spirit I had hoped to land, but what was my disappointment when I found all my dreams dissipated by the noisy boat's-crew filling the *Idler*, one of the brig's boats. There was little time for reflection, or opportunity to indulge in flights of fancy, with these jolly shipmates so eager for a day's freedom on shore, and as a party we set out for an inland tramp. We scrambled for hours through deep chasms, and over steep cliffs — up almost perpendicular mountain sides, until at last we reached the highest traveled point of the highest mountain on the island, and there we stood on an elevation of about two thousand feet above sea level.

Above us reared a conical-shaped peak, in places overhanging and impassable. From here a view of mountains, valleys and the surrounding sea circling the horizon, undotted by a sail, recalled for an instant Robinson's exile. Perhaps from this very spot he had futilely watched for some vessel to appear, on that limitless ocean. It certainly was wild enough even to satisfy *my* imagination of the isolation of Crusoe. But at my elbow, a fellow was daring me to climb the thousand-foot high pinnacle; others were attempting to scale it, which they succeeded in doing for a few feet only, and the reality at hand completely wiped out the earlier image of my boyhood.

On our descent, we stopped to rest under the shadow of a cabbage palm. It had, perhaps, a score of long, graceful leaves, that made a very grateful shade. After looking at the slim, and apparently fragile fronds of the tree, and thinking of it as typical of the tropics, we decided to cut it down. One of our crew had a sheath-knife, and with a few gashes he quickly brought it to the ground, felling the trunk as easily as though it had been what its name suggested — a cabbage. After some rough sport — storming each other with cabbage balls made from the spongy pulp of the tree, the party started again on the return trip. By this time all were a set of noisy, boisterous chaps — shouting, skylarking, making bets as to who was the best man — who could make the fastest time to certain points, either up or down grade. James Ryder, a Georgetown boy, who was quite an athlete, bet he could out-run all of us, in reaching an old stump some distance down the mountain side, and without waiting for a reply he started! His first few steps were fair enough, but from steps they quickly became strides — from six to ten feet apart; when his legs becoming useless to him in so headlong a flight, he fell into the position of a right angle; — with body erect, and legs extended horizontally in front, at intervals trying to check the mad descent. His impetus was so great flying heels would not act as brakes, though they ploughed deep furrows into the soil, and raised a cloud of dust of which his dimly seen body seemed a more solid center.

On he went, faster and faster, until, of a sudden, all was still! the race had come to an end! Down we hurried after! Below must lay a disjointed body! But, when we reached him far beyond the object of the goal, he was already gathering himself together, so to speak, and staggering to uncertain feet, stammered, "hand over, I'm the best man." No one disputed his claim to having won his bet.

After congratulating Ryder on his miraculous escape, we retraced our steps to the shore, somewhat sobered by the adventure. There the boat was waiting for us, and we arrived at the brig in time for dinner. Dinner disposed of, all were soon ready for another visit to the island, this time to gather fruit. With bags and baskets we started for the fertile little valleys, through the nearest pass in the hills. Here we found fruit in abundance, growing wild, and free to be gathered. I never saw more delicious peaches. We climbed into the trees, shaking down those we could not reach, and filling our baskets and bags to over-flowing. While busy with the picking, John Hardy Noyes of Newburyport, belonging to another ship, and I, were in the same tree, when I called his attention to one of the largest peaches I had ever seen hanging just over his head. It was too big for any of our pockets. We thought it the king of peaches, but on getting to the ground, there laid one under the same tree still larger. This island really has the correct soil and atmosphere for the peach. On the same tree are blossoms and fruit, which proves that in the proper climate the peach produces two crops a year.

A warm welcome awaited us on the brig, when we appeared with our heaping baskets and bulging bags of fruit. At the time of the departure of the *General Worth* from Juan Fernandez, we had stored about the deck, fully fifty bushels of fine peaches.

As all necessary supplies now have been taken aboard, and everything is ready for another sea voyage, we shall, without doubt, leave this charming little spot tomorrow if the elements favor. I should like to prolong my stay here for weeks. It has been a "bit of heaven" to us all! Suddenly escaping from old blusterer "Horn," and all his accomplices, and merciless chums, into a little paradisian isle, seemingly dropped from heaven to brighten our way! I cannot join with Crusoe when he is made to exclaim :

> "Better dwell in the midst of alarms,
> Than to reign in this horrible place."

But rather with him would say :

> "I am monarch of all I survey,
> My right there is none to dispute,
> From the center all round to the sea,
> I am lord of the fowl and the brute."

But we will not charge Crusoe with all that the poem credits him with saying. It is more Cowper than Robinson. Alexander Selkirk landed here at his own request, and remained an exile and hermit for four years, when he was finally rescued. He was a Scotchman by birth, — an officer on a British ship; he differed with the captain, and at his own request was taken to this isle in the sea, and left here. But I realize what a wide distinction there is between the genuine and the ideal hermit. I pursued the ideal, but in tracing the real hermitage, I may have lost something of the filmy stuff painted by fancy, that every normal boy feels, but does not try to explain or even understand, awakened by the thought of the thrill of adventure.

This forenoon the ship *St. Mary* of New York, and the *Columbus* of New London, came into the outer harbor, and sent boats ashore for news and supplies, having obtained these, they put to sea again.

Saturday, March 9th. Squally, with rain. Today our neighbors put out to sea, and we soon followed them, favored by squalls coming from the mountains. Though severe, they were behind us, and soon carried us well on our way north. We are on our way again, lessening the distance between us and the "Gates," we are all so eager to enter. "Gold!" the cry we had for a time almost forgotten, is again on everybody's tongue! But, for myself, the memory of that beautiful island in the Pacific will ever remain with me.

Chapter VI

THE DRIFTING DERELICT

Tuesday, March 12th. Lovely weather, still favored by the southeast trades, and making fine progress toward San Francisco. We have studding-sails set on both sides, and are going eight knots an hour, with everything cheerful inboard, and favorable out. This makes sea life attractive, even more, there is a charm to it under these conditions. Were the ocean always so pacific as it is today there would be no trouble in shipping crews. We are still steering a northwest by north course.

Thursday, March 14th. The trades continuing in our favor, we are making fine progress; though not rushing, yet the brig is making good time in the right direction. This afternoon the wind became much lighter, and the ocean calm. Now, the vessel moves so little that she appears like a fixed object on the face of the water. This brings out the fair weather sailors. All hands (passengers) aloft, but two, these brave boys have not yet ventured above the rail. Today crossed the tropic of Capricorn in Longitude 84°, which again brings us into the torrid zone. Still steering a northwest by north course, with all light sails set.

Monday, March 25th. Light winds and very warm weather. Passed through large schools of bonito. This afternoon saw an object rising and falling with the waves, about eight miles distant, which by the glass proved to be a dory. Her sides were covered with sea-grass, and sea-birds were flying around her. We advised the captain to change the course of the brig, and lay for the boat, as yet there might be time to save some unfortunate cast-away. But this he sternly refused to do! — to either change the course of the vessel, or to lower a boat!

He explained, "If I change the course, with these light, baffling winds, we loose at least four or five hours. To try to reach her by the boat would be too risky. A high wind, or sudden squall might spring up — they are frequent in these latitudes — and where would the crew be? They then would be in as bad a fix as that stranded boat there. No, we must pass her!"

Very reluctantly we obeyed the captain, and watched that small derelict drifting in the ocean current, which was stronger than the wind, until it was lost in the distance; the unanswered and unexpressed question of our hearts "what tragedy of the sea did we leave unsolved?" for many years rising, like a phantom that would not be laid, to distress us.

To-day, passed a fore-and-after, steering a north, northwest course. At noon our Latitude was 0° 28'. Longitude 94° 55', our course still northwest by north.

Tuesday, March 26th. Light winds from southwest. This afternoon crossed the Equator in Longitude 95° 00'. The trades have left us, and we are taking advantage of the changeables as they come — light, fresh, fair or calm. We watch the "cat's paws" as they pass ,and whistle for them — sometimes get them — sometimes do not. Much of the time the sails are hanging flat, and useless, and the men are squaring the yards, or trimming sails to take advantage of every little puff of air.

Saturday, March 30th. Fine westerly breeze and rainy. In the afternoon clouds hung dark and heavy, with frequent flashes of lightning. Yesterday saw a schooner about ten miles distant steering north. She is still in sight, and she, like ourselves, is preparing for heavier weather by shortening sail. We have taken in main royal. Our latitude at noon 8° 57' north, Longitude 97° 53'. Course, the best we can do and get out of the bafflings.

Sunday, March 31st. Our heavy weather did not reach us, instead it is warm and pleasant. The passengers and crew are taking advantage of the calm sea by having a swim. This is the last day of March. It has been quite a favorable month with us. Much kinder than the New England blusterer Bryant so well describes in verse:

"The stormy March has come at last,
    With wind, and wave, and stormy skies.
I hear the rushing of the blast
    That through the stormy valley flies."

We are now in the North Pacific, about six hundred miles from the Equator, expecting soon to fall in with the northeast trades. At noon our Latitude was 10° 09' north, Longitude 97° 47' west, course full and by.

Monday, April 1st. Commenced calm and remained

so until late in the afternoon, when we were visited by a severe rain-storm, but it gave us due notice of its coming. Curling black clouds, and black waters driven before them were the sure warning of the approach of the whirlwind. When it struck we were all prepared. There had been time to take in flying jib, royals, topgallant sails, and all lighter sails. However, the hurricane was soon over, and again we were setting sail to a fine northwest breeze, under a clear, blue sky. This is New England's merry day — All Fools Day. At noon Latitude 11° 30' north, Longitude 98° 37' west.

Monday, April 8th. Our run north has been what is considered an average voyage from Juan Fernandez. The winds have been favorable. On Thursday last passed through large schools of porpoises, and succeeded in striking the irons into one of them, but not in securing him. He tore away and escaped followed by the whole school, and we saw no more of them. On Friday large flocks of boobies (a stupid looking sea bird) were hovering over, and occasionally alighting on our yards and rigging. One of them made a roost of the fore yardarm; allowed himself to be captured and brought to the deck, but we were soon as willing to restore to him his freedom as he was to receive it. His excrement became very obnoxious, and we restored him to what he most needed — water. Then we watched the flock until, from mere specks, they finally vanished from sight in the distance.

Chapter VII

REDWOODS UPON THE SEA

On Saturday last sighted the coast of Mexico. Tack ship and stood to the west southwest. The captain says the land is about fifteen hundred miles from Tehuantepec. At noon by observation we were eighteen hundred and fifty miles from San Francisco.

Passengers are busy over-hauling tents, tools and shore gear to be used in the mines; that is, if we ever get there. Everything looks favorable for it today. This afternoon came the second exhibition of the "California Tin and Wood Band." The leader, Mr. Varney, was all right,— but his band! Mr. Varney, our violinist is a good musician, but the instruments of his band include anything that is hollow, or on which anyone can make a noise. Tin pans, barrels, tubs, buckets, handspikes, whatever makes racket or discord, compose the musical instruments of Mr. Varney's band.

It is said music sounds sweetest coming *over* the water, but surely, the only thing that could have made the discords of this "California Tin and Wood" band sound "sweet" was to hear it going *under* the water.

Tuesday, April 18th. Little has occurred worthy of notice, since the last record. There has been little to break the monotony of sea life — watching the sails that occasionally appear on the horizon by day, and star-gazing by

59

night. Last evening we had one of the most gorgeous sunsets I ever saw. As the sun sank behind the ocean horizon, it left the whole western heavens flooded in a blaze of vermillion, thickly dotted with small, deep blue tradewind clouds, bordered by a golden fringe circling the whole flame, while beneath, the ocean shining and varicolored, seemed like numberless highways to fairy grottos. My pen is not skilful enough to paint that wondrous picture, only that of an artist could portray it in all its glory! Today found our bowsprit working badly. A closer survey finds it sprung; probably started during the severe weather encountered off the Cape, — head-beat seas, with the continual strain of the jibs. Hove to for repairs. In setting up the bobstay found the bolt securing it to the cutwater had also loosened. After a half-day's work making all secure, filled away again with a fresh north northeast wind, which compels us to take a full and by course.

Saturday, April 20th. Cool, with a north and east breeze. At noon by observation we are one thousand and twenty miles from San Francisco; still steering a full and by course, and not making the head we could wish.

Wednesday, April 24th. Wind light from northeast by east, and pleasant weather. The air is warmer today. For some time past it has been quite cool. So much cooler, in fact, that flannels and outside coats have felt very comfortable. When we were in the same latitudes in the Atlantic the weather was uncomfortably hot. The difference in the temperature is undoubtedly caused by the wind blowing steadily from the snow-caps of the Cordilleras. The Pacific, though of so much greater extent than the Atlantic, is milder, the temperature more even, and the winds more regular and certain.

At noon our distance from San Francisco was six hundred and seventy miles, bearing north, 18′ east. The day ends with pleasant weather, and light baffling wind. Our course still full and by. This is my brother Isaac's twenty-first birthday. Your freedom day, my dear boy. May you live to enjoy many another happy birthday, is the wish of your first playmate!

Monday, April 26th. Light wind, with some swell. Again hove to for repairs. The bowsprit though considered all right, still calls for attention. After a few more hours making it secure and sea-worthy, filled away again the best we could for a full and by course. Passed through large schools of black fish, and porpoises all puffing and blowing as though they were sole possessors of the ocean. At noon by observation we are in Latitude 28° 52′ north, Longitude 130° west. Course still full and by.

Saturday, May 4th. Our course like the wind has been vacillating; sometimes for and often against. At times headed for our destined port, and again from it. At times with sheets free, and again with yards sharply braced. Our goal is now over the weather bow bearing north by east two hundred and eighty five miles. By dead reckoning, which we are obliged to use (the sun being veiled) we are in Latitude 34° 52′ north, Longitude 127°, 04′, with a cloudy sky, though, not disagreeable weather. A few days ago saw a monster tree floating past, without doubt, a giant redwood, or it may have been a lofty fir, sent to sea by a landslide or perhaps washed from its companions by some tumultous inundation, of frequent occurrence in the rivers of California and Oregon. They are said to be caused by snow being blocked, then thawing and suddenly flooding the country around. The redwood is a colossal native of California, the fir of Oregon, where it is the loftiest and straightest tree that grows.

Sunday, May 5th. Wind and weather changeable, at times clear, then suddenly changing to rain or disagreeable fog. This forenoon passed more forest giants, some coming so near the brig that we could see the type of the gigantic tree, rising and falling so helplessly on the surface of the sea. Like Columbus, these signs all show us, as the boughs, twigs and floating seaweed revealed to him, that land is not far distant.

Monday, May 6th. All hands on the lookout! San Francisco lies just before us! We crowd the rail to view the "promised land." There it lies! but with all the glamour our wildest enthusiasm can paint it, it is yet only an uninviting stretch of waste land, and sand-banks. On we go, dodging our way into a harbor of which we can see but little, it is so thickly covered with sails, and hulks of all descriptions; — every cut of sail, and every shape of spar surrounds us. There must be close to a thousand vessels at anchor in the bay. We pass Clark's Point, a rocky headland on the north, while lying to the south is a long, high sand-drift, called Rincon Point. Our brig is surrounded by a fleet composed of every grade, and every rig of vessel, representing every nation that has deep water craft. Many strange tongues call from stranger-garbed crews; — a Tower of Babel, with the key to the spirit of all the chaos in the one word "Gold!"

At 10 A. M. dropped the *Idler* that last broke ground in the harbor of Juan Fernandez, and our voyage of one hundred and fifty-nine days from Newburyport comes to an end.

Chapter VIII

THE SAN FRANCISCO OF '50

With the arrival of the *Gen. Worth* at San Francisco, the journal of the four years passed in California and Oregon is not kept in chronological order. There were periods when the strenuous life of the young gold-seeker prevented the jotting down of daily occurrences, but not for any great length of time was the record laid aside. He apparently turned to the notes, as one would turn to a confidant; something that always received, if it did not respond to, his recitals of thrilling and unwonted encounters in a primitive country. The author begins the story of his mainland experiences with the first day on shore.

THIS afternoon all went ashore, looking over the city (?) and its surroundings. It was the general opinion that the place had few attractions — a mass of wooden hovels and cloth tents, pitched without order on sand-banks, and what few rocks were not sand covered, on its northern and middle slopes. People from all parts of the world are here, and every language seems to be spoken, but the babel resolves itself into one great motive "Gold, Gold!" and still "Gold!" whatever may be the cost to get it. The climate is good. The mornings now are calm and warm, sometimes even hot, while the afternoons are tempered by strong breezes from the ocean. These winds at times become almost gales, driving the sand before them so forcibly that it is uncomfortable to be out of doors. The winters we are told by old settlers are very different from the springs and summers — rainy and disagreeable with everything at a standstill.

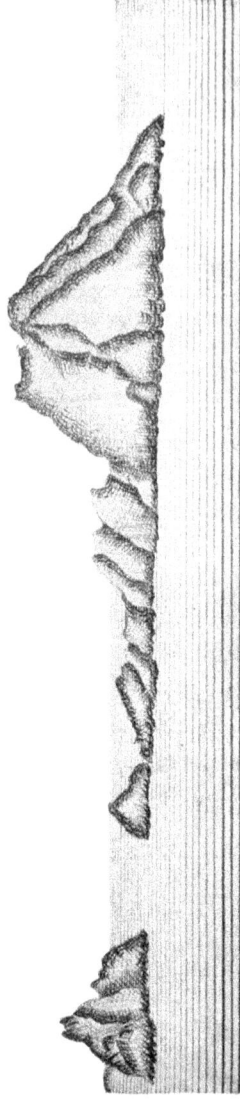

GOAT ISLAND, OFF ISLAND OF JUAN FERNANDEZ

Everyone here is active, and the individual seems to pass for just what he is — stands for his true self. We saw a parson at the hardest kind of manual labor, shoveling, and loading his barrow with stones and dirt, while apparently the roughest type of laborer, was spouting from a platform on political and social rights; the "home banker," with his pick, shovel and pan, bound for the mountains, and the hard handed sailor weighing out gold. Here the old order of things in the east seems to be reversed.

Two other boys and I have decided to build a shack on Telegraph Hill, overlooking the sand-bank that runs out to the bay.

There is a lapse in the diary between the building of the rude shelter, and the first job of work, which, like most pioneer gold seekers, does not take the young adventurer into the mines. He must eat, and that was a very expensive thing to do in those early days in California, necessarily the work at hand was the thing to accept.
The notes again take up the thread of the story.

This afternoon picked up my first job of work, and secured one for a shipmate, Anthony Knapp, a schoolmate of mine at home. We were employed for several weeks, and received ten dollars a day each. This was so encouraging that Anthony and I looked for another job, and soon found it to our sorrow! The same amount was offered us to pull down some shacks that were partially destroyed by fire. They were still hot, but we kept at it, working all through the night. In the morning when presenting our bills, we were told to go to a place (if we can believe what we hear about it) for our pay, much hotter than that in which we had worked for the past twenty-four hours. That was our only recompense for that long night of effort. However, there was plenty of work to be had, and very high wages were given for day's labor, and honest work usually was honestly rewarded.

One day, not long after our unfortunate experience, I was standing just outside our shanty, while my two comrades who shared the shack with me were somewhere near by. Suddenly from the direction of the bay, between the hill and shore, came a puff of smoke. I did not pay much attention to it at first, but even as I looked the smoke grew in volume, until without warning, tongues of flame shot out in several directions, and in less time than it takes to write of it, a raging, rolling, whirlwind of fire was tearing through the tent city, gathering terrific impetus from the strong wind urging it onward. Bells rang! Men went rushing down the hillside, and joining the excited crowd, I, too, ran on in the direction of the fire with the hope that I might be of some help, together with the others, in extinguishing it! The flames were utterly beyond control! The dry cloth of the tents, the flimsy wooden shacks, caught and burned like tinder, while the strong wind lashed the flames before it, until there was nothing more for it to gorge its all consuming appetite upon. In a very short time the crude mining town was a thing of the past! Only smoking heaps of ashes, and charred débris told where San Francisco had stood, for the town had burned to the very sand on which the mushroom miners' structures had pushed upward.

That evening we three boys met in our little home on

Telegraph Hill. Our shanty, with a few others, had escaped the fire! The heights had not been swept, the elevation undoubtedly, protecting it from the reach of the flames. Below us lay a smoking, ashy waste, flat to the sand, while the gold-seekers were shelterless as at first, to begin all over. And this they did with a will! The second San Francisco rose more substantially constructed than that first city of tents and hovels.

The young adventurer was now to have his mettle tried to the utmost. A catastrophe greater than anything he had yet known, was to befall him. The frozen specters of Cape Horn he had eyed "breast forward," with steady and firm heart, for he possessed rugged health. Now, he was to meet a new problem, more to be dreaded than any previous one, for the odds were against him.

Shortly after the burning of the city, the awful tragedy called "the Plague" laid many of the shelterless fire-victims low. The dead and dying were on all sides! The death cart made its morning visits to collect those who had died during the night, and many were buried without funeral rites, in heaped furrows of unknown dead. Many boys who had gone so bravely to seek their bags of gold, were never to be heard from back in the New England towns!

The three boys in the shack on Telegraph Hill were smitten, and for days no entry was made in the journal. When Richard was well enough to be around again, he writes: —

Chapter IX

THE PLAGUE FOLLOWING THE FIRE

THESE last few weeks, confined in this little hut, thus out from the world, have been the most unhappy of my whole life. Three pent-up boys, who have known little of sickness, and less of the world, crowded into an eight by twelve inclosure, not so good as some of our New England hen pens for size and comfort: — doctor's patients, acting as their own cooks and nurses, seldom seeing faces other than their pale, cadaverous ones, at times delirious — is the sad picture I draw of these once ambitious, but now discouraged gold-seekers. But why complain? There are many around us more unfortunate than us — sick and dying on every hand; some with friends, and some who are friendless, dying and dead, to be gathered up in the morning by the death cart for the graves or the trench.

In our shanty was one door, and a small single window. The door was usually closed. From the window came our only light, and from it also we had a view of the town below, and a curve of the bay beyond. One morning, as I was just getting about again, from the window I was watching a man and his helper, trying to sink a shaft for water through the solid ledge near our shanty. They had already reached the depth of ninety feet, and were still blasting. Day after day they toiled away, with more hope than water, for they well knew if they struck a spring below the rock, they truly would have discovered gold, as good water was in great demand. It was one of the scarce articles and sold as readily as bread or beef.

On this morning the man had taken his position, with his tools, in a big tub or bucket secured by a chain to a cranked windlass. The helper as usual lowering down, had just started a turn perhaps, while the man was standing in the bucket, holding the chain by his hands, just over his head. Suddenly I heard a snap, as of metal breaking, and to my horror, I saw the chain give away three links above his grasp. Then came the sound of the thundering of his car, as it struck the walled sides of the well in its rapid course downward. After that, all was quiet!

I forgot my illness, and rushed out raising the cry "Man killed"!

While a crowd quickly gathered, gear was rigged, and the unfortunate well-sinker brought to the surface. The on-lookers pressed in upon him, crying, "Is he dead?" Was he dead? No, indeed. His knee was slightly injured, but as he was assisted to his feet he grittily stammered, "It was not the fall that hurt, but the sudden stop." All of which goes to prove, that there is humor in almost any situation, if one has the spirit of the philosopher, — and the outcome is favourable.

The following morning I started out for my first walk around the hill, since my sickness. It was a clear, pleasant morning, the air and sky far more agreeable than the scenes around me. Within a half-hour's walk I witnessed signs of terrible suffering. Indeed, we were not the only ones who had fallen under the scourge. Quickly pitched tents, hovels, or whatever offered shelter from the cool evening air, and the heat of the noonday sun, dotted our hillside making a repulsive outlook at every turn. I soon began to retrace my steps, for our hut, bare and uninviting as it might be, was now, at least, the only home of the convalescent. On every hand was want and misery. The plague had taken, and was still taking its deadly toll.

In returning to our shack, I made a complete circuit of the hill. On a barren spot, facing the bay, I came upon a herd of pitiful and famished-looking calves, securely leashed to posts. My heart went out to these bitterly bleating little animals, crying for food and water, and my sympathies prompted me to appease their hunger. As I patted the face of a shy little creature, and was about to give it something to eat, a stranger quickly warned me not to feed it.

"These calves," said he, "belong to Mexican owners, whose business it is to corral and slaughter them for the market. Some of these butchers would have no compunction in slaughtering you for such an act. *These* calves are selected from the big herd you see in the valley yonder," indicating with his hand a spot further inland. "They are kept without food and water to give the veal a whiter color."

As I continued on my way, I had a deep feeling of understanding for these unhappy beasts, for were we not both in sad straits!

In a few days all admitted I was far ahead of my companions on the road to health. This is to be my last week in San Francisco, as the doctor (who has charged us ten dollars for each visit) has prescribed a change of air for me.

On July 8, 1850, the boy boarded the steamer *"Carolina"* headed for Portland, Oregon. He had not yet fully recovered his strength, and was assisted onto the boat by two of his friends, Steven Johnson, and his — Steven's — brother Philip. The journey was a gloomy one, as the effects of the plague were still with them, and one little girl, who was traveling with her parents died on the steamer before reaching port. The journal continues : —

On our way up after passing the headlands, we stopped at Pacific City, Astoria, near the entrance of the Columbia and Vancouver, the old noted trading post of Oregon. We arrived at Portland after a run of seven days from San Francisco.

Chapter X

PORTLAND OREGON IN '50

I FIND Portland to be a small settlement on the banks of the Willamette River, a branch of the Columbia, about twelve miles from its mouth. Only a few whites inhabit the place, and they are mostly western people, while many Indians live on the outskirts of the village. The Indians, who are anything but neat looking, live in wigwams, and their principal food is "moose-e-moose" or deer, and salmon, with whatever they can get from the whites in the shape of odds and ends. They are not at all particular about the condition of what they eat — it may be spoiled, and bad smelling, but they readily devour everything that comes in their way unmindful of age or odour.

The streets are narrow and irregular, and in places quite unsafe for traveling.

Just before the boy reached Oregon, the Chinook Indians and the coast tribes were visited by a terrible scourge, with symptoms like chills and fever. Being unused to the manner of white people, and with childlike ignorance, crediting much that they did not understand to the supernatural, they believed that the "pale face" had caused this sickness to come upon them by the influence of evil spirits. They had seen fire shooting into the air (fireworks on a holiday) and this they believed had been done to blast them with this dreadful sickness.

Their method of getting rid of the disease was by Indian rites, and by plunging into the sea when feeling the heat of the fever. When the chill appeared they jumped into ovens of heated stone, that they had built for the purpose, and there roasted

72

FAIR WEATHER

A CHINOOK CANOE, OREGON

until the chill had passed. Many died, perhaps, from the merciless manner of treating their sufferings. With the appearance
of this disease these tribes began to decline in strength and
numbers.

The young adventurer, again regaining his accustomed good
health, starts for the mines. He writes in the journal:—

I have been in Oregon thirty-seven days, with the exception of a few days spent in a wild-goose chase to the
Klamath mines, and I shall make Portland my home for
a while longer. My first stopping place was the Hanks
and Bodell House. Securing a job in another location, I
soon changed my lodgings to the Baker House, and later
to Hart's, working at whatever came in my way. My
trip into the mines deserves notice. The preceding weeks,
yes, even months had passed, and I had not started upon
the great adventure for which I had come so far. The
cry of "Gold" was in the air, here, as in San Francisco.
It was sweeping over the Columbia valley like a contagion, and all were catching the epidemic.

We formed a company, composed of Waldo Jewett,
William Dinsmore, Stephen Johnson, and myself. Dinsmore and I purchased a white Indian pony, full of vim
and as contrary as a mule. The pony was wholly unused
to packing. We shared alike in the enterprise, and getting
our supplies, packed our beasts, and started in high spirits.
Each horse had a packsaddle, with pads to prevent chaf-
ing, everything secured by a surcingle buckled under his
belly. Within these packs were enormous supplies of provisions, with tools and tents. Over the whole, horse and
pack, was a rope lashing everything securely together.

We had traveled perhaps ten miles when the pony appeared to be getting restless and nervous. His driver, Dinsmore, from the first had been impatient and irritable, and proved that he was wholly unfit to control the horse. Instead of persuasion he applied the lash freely to the overloaded, high-spirited beast, and accompanied this harsh treatment with abuse and cursing. Finally, as if indignant at the continued insults and unfair treatment, the pony stopped. Nothing could urge the angry animal to take another step. He wheeled, heels toward us, and soon gave *us* the strongest reasons for running. His terrible weapons flashed in such rapid succession, we were only too willing to get out of the way. Like lightning, came a storm of dangerous kicks until, at last, the load upon his back became loosened, and hung in an unshapely mass between his hoofs, just within reach of his flying heels.

For a few minutes the air was thick with picks, shovels, tin pans, dried beef, tent gear, and flour — especially flour!

We fled for safety, but were not quick enough to escape the blinding storm of flour, or the frequent thumps of tools, and tent pins, descending in all directions!

Soon all was quiet — the snowstorm had abated — and there we stood, looking for all the world, like two snow images made by boys at play in a New England blizzard, or like frosted figures in a confectioner's showcase. Dinsmore had but little to say, and I still less! What could two rough miners, garbed like angels all in an instant do, but laugh sickly, and make the best of the situation?

We shook the white dust from our garments, gathered up the fragments, made another pack, and started forward again. Just before reaching a resting place, a few miles from the bottom lands of Long Tom, the pony gave us another exhibition of his wonderful agility. In less time than it takes to relate it, his back again was as bare as before packing. This time there was nothing left but a broken mass of the left overs from the first disaster — useless wreckage and junk. Fortunately the flour had all been exhausted at the first kicking. This time everything was ruined utterly, and nothing was left but splinters.

We decided to give up the venture, and return. We sold the pony, and gave the shattered implements to the purchaser, and thus ended our Oregon gold vision! Dinsmore and I awoke from our dream, and we separated never to meet again.

As I watched the pretty little pony being led away by his new owner, I thought I had never seen so lovely a little creature! — white as a lily, and proud as a peacock, with erect head, and wild, flowing mane; quick, nervous, and as keen-sighted as a hare, always giving notice of any moving object on the trail before him, by forward pointed ears, and frequent neighing; fleet and sure-footed as a deer, and affectionate, to a kind master, as a child, he was truly the wild spirit of the trail.

There is danger in buying a horse from the Indians. Their horses are kindly trained by them, and they never forget their old masters. The Indian seldom sells a horse except when traveling, and the pony is as familiar with the habits of the tribe, and the route as the Indian himself. After buying an animal, if the owner does not leash him securely, he may, without warning, find the horse gone. The pony follows the trail of his former master, who aware of his coming, soon sells him to another, and so on, until often when the tribe returns to its starting point, it does so with the full number of horses it had at first.

Arriving in Portland, I went direct to Baker's, and was again soon on the lookout for another job.

My last adventure toward the mines had proved an expensive one — forty dollars lost on the horse alone, besides the complete loss of provisions, tools, and other things that together made quite a sum that I could ill afford to sacrifice. Ten-dollar-a-day jobs were things of the past, and I gladly jumped at one for six. For a time I acted as substitute for a sick steward on the steamer Willamette that ran between Portland and Astoria, and finding nothing else to do, later worked as steward for the California House.

Chapter XI

THE GHOSTLY VISITANT

At the California House were several lumber men, hailing from the state of Maine. One of them seemed to be superior mentally to his mates. He was tall and lank, careless in his dress, quiet in his manner, yet, unlike the others he was not a gold-seeker. He was a born inventor. He tinkered over machinery, puzzled out new methods of constructing houses or boats, and was very original and ingenious. If he had an idea, he followed it out to its completion, no matter what the sacrifice of time, tools or money. It often seemed to me that New England would have been a far more congenial place for one of his type. He always had three or four "irons in the fire", and finished one only to start afresh upon another. He conceived the idea of sawing out a plank twelve feet square. This he soon accomplished; at that time it never had been done. To make the twelve-foot depth, he welded the long up and down saws together. Then he went still further, and sawed a twelve foot *cube*. This proved a masterpiece of ingenuity.

During my stay at the California House I became quite friendly with Peter Loudine, who came from the state of New York. He was the cook, and received the salary of one hundred and fifty dollars per month. We occupied the same room, in which there were two bunks or berths, one above another, as the house was built like all others of the time, after the fashion of a ship, with bunks against the sides of the rooms, sometimes two or three above each other. Peter occupied the upper bunk, and I, the lower one. He was an intelligent boy, quite frank about his affairs, especially those of the heart, and liked to confide in me. He was deeply in love with a young Indian girl, and hoped to marry her before long. She was pretty, and belonged to the Spokane tribe, whose wigwams were just outside the city. She could not speak English, nor he Indian, but this did not interfere with his suit. There apparently was a language, perhaps unspoken, that they both understood. One evening Peter and I were chatting away, he giving me confidences about his sweetheart, when I frankly "gave him a piece of my mind," rating him about his lack of taste in choosing such a wife, so far removed from his own blood. His reply surprised me.

"My mother was a full-blooded Indian. You seem surprised, but it's a fact. So, you see, I am mixed, and my girl has more right than I to find fault — she's a straight breed. I am neither English nor Indian, but I love the Indian race. It's in my blood. Don't try to choose a girl for me. I've made my choice, and if she wants me, she can have me."

Peter was deeply in earnest, his manner left no doubt on the subject, and, though I had not suspected his Indian blood, the fact made rather a strong argument in favour of his selection. After our talk I never referred adversely to his love affair, but sometimes even went with him on his visits to the Indian settlement.

It was about this time that Loudine told me he in-

tended to join a party of men, under the leadership of a
Mr. McKenzie, who were off to plant a settlement farther
down the coast (Cape Orford). His plan was, after he had
established a home for himself, to marry the Indian girl,
and take her there to live. He endeavored to persuade me
to become one of the number, but I had my own reasons
for not entering the venture — my thoughts were again
centered on a return to San Francisco.

I had not seen Peter long enough to speak to him at any
length for several days, as he was busy with his new plans,
and I with mine, when, after returning one evening later
than usual I found him waiting for me. His expression
was so melancholy, and his voice sounded so spiritless,
that I could not fail to notice his unusual manner at
once, and fancied something unfavorable to the settlement down the river had occurred. However, I made no
comment, but promptly joined him in the walk I knew
he was awaiting.

Yet, not at once did Peter begin the confidence I felt
was coming! Usually there was a boyish effervescence in
his manner, that readily found vent in spurts of intimate
self-revealment. Tonight he remained gloomy and taci-
turn. For some time we walked on in silence. Finally
Peter commenced, haltingly,

"Chips," thus he had dubbed me from our first acquaintance "I've got something on my mind that is just
eating me up!"

I looked my interest, but remained silent, and Loudine
continued.

"Whatever you think about what I'm going to tell

you, know that it's God's truth — every word of it! You know me well enough to understand that I have no reason to lie to you."

He glanced frankly at me, and yet there was a certain hesitation as though he feared to be misunderstood. I tried to reassure him, perhaps with some degree of success, for he added,

"Last night my dead sister came into our room and stood just in front of my berth! Her dress brushed the side of your bunk, but it did not crumple, as the folds faded into the shadows.

"Twice before she has come to me, and each time she has foretold the death of one of the family."

I was somewhat startled by this rather remarkable confession, which proved to be of such an entirely different nature from what I had expected. But he seemed not to notice my surprise, and talked on softly, as though thinking aloud.

"The first time she came was at home. Each visit has been one of warning. All in filmy white, she suddenly appeared beside me, and only I saw and heard her speak. When she first came to me, she said, 'sister will join me,' telling the exact day that my only living sister should leave us. Her words came true! My sister was taken ill, and passed away on the very day she predicted.

"Several years later, while on shipboard at sea, she came again. Those around me did not see her. But I saw her, and heard the tones of her voice. This time she told the manner, and day of our mother's death, and when our ship docked, there the news of her death awaited me."

Brig General Worth "Lying to" in a Gale, in the Pacific Ocean, Off Strait of Magellan

Brig General Worth "Lying to" in a Gale Off River La Platte

Peter's voice died almost to a whisper, as though re-
calling the sorrow of that message, and the sad events
that followed.

"Chips," he added, turning to me, so earnestly that
had I been inclined to doubt the truth of the story, I at
least knew he sincerely believed in his vision.

"Chips, last night she came again! She has given *me*
the warning. I am the next to go! No, no, don't doubt it.
I was awake. As much awake as I am at this very minute.
She said 'brother, our circle is soon to be rounded. You
will join us next, and then we shall all be together!' She
looked down at you, and added, 'this young man will be
very sick, but he will recover, and return to his home.'
It will all be as my sister has predicted. She has never
been mistaken. My days are numbered!"

The impression was branded indelibly on Peter's mind,
and it was of no avail to endeavor to combat it.

Now, the day of the departure down the coast drew
near. Peter Loudine said good-by to his Indian sweetheart, telling her as best he could that he should send for
her soon. But to me he told a very different story.

"I shall never marry the girl" — squaw, he called her
— "for I shall soon be in the happy hunting ground."

Nevertheless, while I pooh-poohed, his gloomy state
of mind, there hung over things, even the expedition, as
far as Peter's share entered into it, a sense of foreboding
and depression, that proved anything but reassuring.

The group of adventurous young men under the command of Mr. McKenzie arrived at the spot they had decided upon for a settlement, and began to cut the logs to

be used in erecting a rude fort, or place of protection from the Indians. A tribe of red men had recently been on the warpath in this part of the wilderness, and had committed many indignities and outrages upon wandering whites, and for this reason Mr. McKenzie's little band had been warned to take great precautions.

The details of the expedition were related to me some weeks later : —

The building of the fcrt progressed quickly enough, but it had not yet been completed, and made secure enough to protect them, when one cloudy night, the keen eye of a hunter glimpsed bushes swaying in a rather more violent manner than that caused by the wind. He knew at once what stirred the branches, behind the small trees, at no great distance from the incompleted fort. He went at once to Mr. McKenzie, and said,

"That ain't no wind. Them's Indians! The tribe is on the warpath, they're waiting here for the rest to join 'em, then they 'll make an attack. They out-number us ten to one. Not a soul will get out with his life, if we wait for the whole tribe to come down on us."

Mr. McKenzie called the men about him and told them his plan. Fortunately the wind had risen, and clouds had rolled up, making the night dark as a pocket. Later on, it began to rain, and the sound of the wind and rain, both aided the leader in the course he had mapped out. In the height of the storm, every man stole out of the fort en-closure, as silently as wild creatures of the night, some crawling along on hands and feet, until they reached the shore. Here the party entered the water, that the Indians might lose their trail, and for miles walked through the pounding surf, with the rain descending upon their heads, and the waves dark and surging beneath their feet. When they thought their footsteps sufficiently obscured, they again came upon the shore, and entered the woods, following the coast until they reached Portland.

Word had been received by the inhabitants that Mr. McKenzie and his boys were on their way back. A friendly Indian had carried the word ahead, and also the story of the tragedy they so fortunately had escaped.

All Portland turned out to greet Mr. McKenzie and his returning company. And when they found all the members were safe, there was a rousing welcome.

Peter Loudine came with them, but he of all the others had received a wound upon the knee, by the glancing blow of an axe. It seemed simple enough at first, when suddenly blood poisoning developed, and within a few days the apparition's prophesy had come true. Peter had joined the family circle in the land of the unknown.

The loss of Peter was a distinct blow to me. I did not try to solve the mysterious circumstances of his death. He so absolutely believed in the sentence apparently received from a source beyond the knowledge of mortals, that, it may be explained, when he really did fall sick he had not the courage to combat it. However, in the rugged and active life here on the Pacific coast, the events of yesterday, no matter of what moment, are speedily crowded out by those of today. We soon ceased to speak of Peter Loudine, as other interests forced him, for the moment, from our minds.

Chapter XII

THE WARNING COMES TRUE

OCTOBER 1ST, 1852. I have now been in Portland for nearly fifteen months, and have seen many changes. The tide of immigration has poured in from all parts of the west, while men of many trades and occupations, to me, seem to be over crowding the place. They are pushing in both by land and sea. During these months the first river steamer has been launched, — it was the *Lot Whitcomb*, built at Milwaukee, a few miles up the river — The first printing press landed in Portland, and was welcomed by the booming of guns, great cheering of enthusiastic crowds, and rousing speeches. A few days later I read the first copy of the "Oregonian," the first paper published in Oregon. The editor is said to come from Ohio. Among the compositors in the office was Alfred Berry, a Newburyport man, who had served his apprenticeship on the "Newburyport Herald," and had graduated at the same time with my brother Enoch.

Many months had passed since the *Gen. Worth* sailed from Newburyport, with Richard determined to seek his fortune in the gold mines of the Pacific Coast. Yet in all these months he had not made one successful venture into the mines. The journal gives no satisfactory explanation, in fact the young man does not seem to note the delay to his unfulfilled visions, other than philosophically to accept whatever turn fortune's wheel presents to him. As the pioneer, he had felled big trees, worked at erecting the primitive shelters for the gold-seekers; as cook on a river steamer, and at the California House, and the journal implies that whatever kind of work offered, he gladly accepted, but into the mines he had never really penetrated.

One trip toward the mines had met with absolute disaster, yet he still remained on the coast, perhaps hopeful that some day success might be his. Finally he decides to forsake Oregon and again return to San Francisco. But before leaving, he visits a friend living on the prairies, and there sees the original forests, and unexplored valleys in all their native grandeur.

I wished to see the great firs of Oregon, — the trees that had welcomed us on our arrival, rising so futile and so prone upon the waters of the ocean. The finest specimens grow on the river banks, bordering the high prairie lands. The upper stretches of the prairies lie between the banks, and the low pasture lands, used only as feeding grounds for cattle. The soil of the high prairie is undoubtedly the most fertile in the entire territory. The bordering banks of the rivers are higher, but less rich and productive, and here grow the colossal firs. Whole forests pierce the clouds, some of their tops reaching up to a height of two hundred feet, straight as a ship's mast, and great in girth — not one misshapen or distorted. I have walked among this court of kingly trees, and felt awed and lost within their dominion. No other country in the world produces such magnificent firs as Oregon.

The great forests flank the prairies: first the fertile high lands, very productive when cultivated; in primitive condition, often covered with a grass rank and coarse frequently growing to a height of six or seven feet, then beyond them lie the pastures low and green, and flower-decked.

Before leaving Oregon I came into this section to visit a

friend, and although while here I conracted the "shakes," as chills and fever is called in this section, I was repaid by seeing the wildness and majesty, and the limitless spaces of this boundless country. These higher, or between lands, as they are called, are unhealthy, and miasmatic or intermittent fevers prevail, and it was while here that I contracted the illness, which, however, did not make its appearance until my return to Portland.

Through the vast woods range all kinds of game, and over the free stretches of green prairie flit quail, pheasants, wood ducks, partridges, wild pigeon and birds of many species. Wild geese, and swans linger here in their migratory season. The geese feed openly all day upon the ponds, and lakes of the prairie, but the swans are more timid, and only at night drop down to find their food at the bottom in the shallow waters.

So unafraid of man are the animals, that I have seen a hungry wolf, in broad daylight, chase a deer within half a rifle shot of our camp. Out into the open they ran, the wolf not at all deterred from his pursuit by the noise of the company so close at hand.

What an untamed and untried country this is! What possibilities await capital and energy combined, to make use of the splendid forests and the fertile soil. I am glad to have had a glimpse into this primitive region before leaving it, and while I may not have filled my sack with gold-dust, the trip to Portland has been worth while in many ways, and I would not have foregone the experience.

Upon my return I developed the attack of "shakes," which fortunately did not last long, but they were uncomfortable enough while engaged in "shaking" me. It was then I recalled the prophesy of Peter Loudine's night visitant. Poor Peter! There is something very weird about the memory of his ghostly interviews and the accuracy with which their prophesies came true. Perhaps, had his sentence been so light as mine, his illness would not have proved fatal. But why speculate?

> "There are more things in heaven and earth, Horatio,
> Than are dreamt of in your philosophy."

So Hamlet tells us, and we must needs agree with him.

Again San Francisco is to be my destination. After bidding good-by to my new made friends, and all things being ready, I embarked on the brig, *Tarquina*, and was soon on my way down the river. After a favourable run to the lower anchorage, we met with rough weather, and lay at anchor all night while a heavy gale prevented us from leaving until well into the morning.

On Monday, October 13th, the *Tarquina* entered the Golden Gate, after a passage of thirteen days from Portland, and anchored in the bay off the city. It is with the feeling that I am not a stranger, but rather returning as one of the early settlers, that I am again approaching San Francisco. There are fewer craft around us than at my first entry, and from a distance, it would seem that many changes have taken place on the shore.

Chapter XIII

SAN FRANCISCO IN '52

THE following morning we landed, and took a stroll about the city; but seek as we might there was nothing to remind us of the San Francisco of fifteen months before. From the ashes of the fire, another town had arisen, in some respects much better than the early one of tents and shanties, the streets more closely followed a definite plan, and there were several very good buildings, with fewer tents, still, it was yet a very primitive place, with a population composed mainly of men, bearded, and clothed in the roughest attire.

I climbed Telegraph Hill and sought the small building in which we three boys lived during those first months, and in which we weathered the storms of pestilence and fire. But now, nothing remained even to tell of the old site. Somewhere near the spot a larger, and somewhat more solidly constructed structure stood. I turned, as I had once months before, when a blazing landscape flamed below me. Now, a more substantially built city lay between me and the beautiful waters of the bay, still crude, but, giving real promise, and rising with more solidity, that bespoke enduring purpose for the future. While crossing Happy Valley I met a friend of the earlier days. During our talk he told me that quite a colony of Newburyporters were now located in San Francisco. I hunted up these men from the old home town, and soon became one of them, for among them were several boyhood friends.

For a few weeks I worked, as did all the others, at whatever happened to present itself; assorting lumber, pile-driving, harbor lightering, whatever work was at hand. Then there came an opportunity to try the mines again, and I was soon on the river steamer *Confidence* on the way to Marysville.

On board there were a jolly lot of passengers. Always on joining a new company of people, I looked about me, and took "account of stock" as it were, of my companions. On the *Confidence*, the leader and wit of the party was a tall Kentuckian, who claimed to be a lawyer and ex-member of Congress. He was the tallest man I ever saw. His garments were of the coarsest homespun, cut in a curious style, reaching in one piece from his ankles to his shoulders, where they were held in place by shoulder-straps. This covered a flannel shirt, which was partly concealed by a rakish looking little jacket, while a broad-brimmed hat, with heavy, high boots, into which his pants were tucked, began and ended his regalia. His hair and beard were long, and thickly sprinkled with gray, and when the slouched hat was removed, it disclosed a nobly moulded head, while beneath a commanding brow, shone the steady eyes of the leader. While his garments were ludicrous, and extremely rough, his voice and manner revealed him to be a man of education, and a certain courtly bearing, confessed him to be of a different station than that to which the queer rig belonged.

He gave his name as Allen, and said he was a descend-

ant of Col. Ethan Allen, of revolutionary fame, and that
his grandfather emigrated from Vermont to Kentucky in
1784. As he sat in the center of an interested group, towering above us all in stature, I could not but think, listening to his quick responses to would-be wags, or replying
to questions of state affairs, that here also he towered
mentally above us all. This man was a fighter, like his
ancestor, but not a fighter with brawn or powder, his
brain was his great weapon, and here he had collected
ammunition to vanquish his enemies, or re-inforce his
vanquished party. A remarkable character clad so out-
landishly, yet openly confessing to a nobility he could not
conceal! He was going into the mines like the rest of us
to discover gold.

Every country, and every class, is represented here on
board the *Confidence*, journalists and laborers, profession-
als, and mechanics, and there is also a band of singers.
The leader is a young German, who speaks very good
English. His company were seated on settees on the
hurricane deck, just forward the wheel-house, while he
occupied a stool in front of them, quite near the rail, and
the passengers who had been attracted by the singing, and
were joining in the merry choruses, were crowding in
upon them. Song after song had floated out over the
water, and been lost among the stars of the dark night,
when we demanded that the young leader sing us a solo.
This he did in a musical tenor; other songs followed, very
sweet love ballads, when he said "Now, boys, I will give
you one other — then I 'm done."

He began; the song was "Bonapart's Grave," and we

were listening intently, for it was a treat to hear so good a voice, and so good a musician was unusual in these parts, when without warning the steamer gave a great lurch! She had run into a bank in a sudden turn, causing the lurch and a list to starboard. The young singer was standing near the rail, and he received the whole force of the shock of the impact. He was hurled overboard, striking the low rail with his feet, and making a complete somersault sank from sight under the driving-wheel!

The steamer was backed, life buoys thrown out, boats launched, but we could find no trace of the body of the sweet singer. He sang his swan song, and disappeared forever! Another steamer just in our wake joined us in the search, and for a long time we remained in the neighborhood, but we sought in vain, and then, with great regret we steamed forward on our way. It was a tragic ending to our pleasant evening. The singer was a stranger to everyone, even the members of his company knew little about him. They had met, then common interests had kept them together. So it ever is here in this new country, nothing is asked or known of the stranger, but his present standing and the attraction or need of the moment.

A deep gloom settled over the boat's company, but an hour before so full of rollicking cheer and pleasure. It seemed to me that of all those present the old Kentuckian seemed most deeply touched by the loss of the young man.

Chapter XIV

THE ROBBER—AN OFFER TO GO INTO BUSINESS

AFTER reaching Marysville I entered one of the first Hotels (?) on my way, and booked for the night. The building was a rough affair, with low posted sides, covered with poor siding; unfinished, knotty boards for flooring, and long, western rift shingles for roofing. It is the custom here when coming unknown to a new place to register one's name, birthplace, and destination, then friends following later may know where one is bound, and find one in case they so desire.

I had just finished writing my name, with the usual information, when I heard a voice exclaiming in a low tone beside me,

"Well, friend, I'm glad to see you again. Which way are you traveling, up or down?"

"Up" and "Down," were common localisms, meaning the "up" or "down" of the river, or the mountains, whichever made the lay of the land.

"Up," I replied in a not too cordial voice, for I had noticed this man on the steamer, and had rather avoided him, while I saw that he followed me with his eye continually. Then he said, "That is my direction."

It was with a certain repugnance that I now felt that he was following me. He was of medium height, with a well-knit frame, and he was fairly good-looking, but there was something sinister in his eye, as it trailed after me. Apparently he was attracted toward me, yet was puzzling for some reason, over an unsettled mental question. Perhaps he had the unfounded idea that I possessed nuggets which, he thought would feel very comfortable in his pockets. Whatever the case, I didn't like his looks, and wished to avoid him.

The next morning I was just starting on my way to Rose Bar, having almost forgotten the interview of the night before, when up walked Buck—he had signed his name on the hotel register as Walter Buck. He was already to begin his journey, but had a much quicker, and easier one mapped out than that which I had planned. It was a short cut, which would save time, and stage hire, but would bring us into a very lonely part of the woods, — *so I took a stage*, a rough concern, more resembling a hayrack than a stagecoach, and Buck proceeded to walk. We had not traveled more than five miles, when the conveyance was stopped by two men, and one of them was Walter Buck. He at once recognized me by a nod of the head, and introduced his companion as he climbed into the hayrack, which he had been so eager to avoid in the start.

I was now rather irritated at what, very evidently, was no chance meeting. This man undoubtedly was following me. For what reason I could only suspect. After a drive of perhaps twenty miles, we reached Long's Bar, the stage with Buck's companion turned onto another road, and I got out to walk the five miles up the river to Rose Bar. But I did not begin that walk alone, for I was no sooner down from the wagon, than with some explanations Buck also alighted, and followed on the trail either beside or behind me. After being ferried across the Yuba River, we entered the trail that climbed the steep river bank, and led on to a narrow footpath continuing through thick woods. About half way from the banks of the stream to the hill country, we came to a higher level, along which the path crawled after reaching the higher altitude, still through thick woods. Buck loitered after reaching this isolated section, often turning around and calling my attention to the grandeur of the scenery. Thus we had gone on, until about half way to Rose Bar, when suddenly he stopped, and said.

"I'm going to sit down in the woods for a smoke. Won't you join me?"

I declined, and stayed in the open, for by this time I had grown very suspicious, and I had seen in his belt a bowie, and a five shooter. If he intended robbery or murder I intended to sell out as dearly as possible, although I had not even a jackknife as a weapon of defence. Coming out onto the trail again, we continued along the path, he keeping the same slow jog, and I cautiously falling back in the rear.

We had gone on in this manner for a short distance, when he slowly lessened the space between us until he was by my side. Then I decided to bring the farce — if so it proved to be — to a climax.

"Now," I said, "who and what are you? Why have you been dogging my steps since we left San Francisco?" I looked him squarely in the eye, watching alertly for any sudden move on his part, but well knowing that good brawn and muscle could avail but little if called to battle with his weapons. He returned my glance, with something of a threat lurking in his dark eyes, that his words did not express, for they were civil enough.

"Do you suspect me, friend?"

"I do!" There was a pause tense with feeling on my part, as I answered, for I well knew that I had forced this climax, and must take the consequences.

"Of what do you suspect me?" he parried.

"Never mind; why you have followed me, and your motives are best known to yourself, but I have had enough of this farce. Now, what do you want?"

His glance lowered, and I fancied a smile of satisfaction flitted for a second across his face, then as though some question had been definitely settled, he swung into the same quick pace in the lead, with,

"Feel uneasy no longer, friend, I will do you no harm." He continued well ahead of me until we reached Rose Bar, but there I lost sight of him when I booked at a rude miners' house for the night, and with a feeling that I was well rid of an unwelcome companion, I quickly went to bed, and was soon fast asleep, for the day had been a hard one.

But Walter Buck was not to be disposed of so lightly. In the morning he appeared again. He had really remained at the house overnight, and he continued there for several days longer. Just before leaving, this strange fellow came to me and asked if I would accompany him to a small valley just over a nearby hill. If this was another ruse I would show him that I was not afraid of him, and we walked on, until I saw that the valley was hill-locked in all directions, but that in which we had entered.

One might almost have fancied the hollow had been quarried from the granite ledges encircling it, but for the sloping pass through which we had entered. Nothing stirred within the wind protected enclosure, and an absolute silence reigned. I had again taken no weapon with me, and had he any evil intention upon my life, he could very well here in this lonely place kill and rob me, and the deed would never be discovered. But I had no fear of this man. My attitude was rather one of surprise, mingled with a certain curiosity to see what new move he would make.

"Friend, sit down," he pointed to a flat rock near at hand. I did as he suggested, and he seated himself near me.

"I have brought you to this quiet spot, to speak to you without fear of being overheard," he continued. His speech was a queer mingling of refinement bred in the east, with exclamations and expressions caught from the rough life on the coast.

"Now, this company — what do you expect from it? Do you know it is near bankruptcy? That water-wheel you were inspecting yesterday — they cannot pay fifty per cent on what it has cost to put it into position. If you have bought stock in the company, you never will get any return to speak of. Perhaps you do not believe me. It is part of my business to keep posted about the color that goes out from the mines. This claim is about played out."

ALBATROSS ON A ROCK

SWAN

ALBATROSS SITTING ON THE WATER

MOTHER CAREY'S CHICKEN,
OR STORMY PETREL

DRAWINGS OF SEA BIRDS

I imagined there was a double meaning, or some sinister fact implied by his last sentence. But I made no reply, neither accepting what he had said nor rejecting it — letting the play go on to the finish. Seeing that he had not sufficiently convinced me, he brought up more arguments.

"Friend, what can you expect if all goes well? As I 've told you, the claim's played out, — that I know. Little dust has been cleared up for some time. I've got something *worth while* to offer you. In no time at all you 'll clear up enough to get out with, and give up the business if you want to. Now, see here, I 've followed you clear from 'Frisco, to size you up, — to make sure you had the stuff in you I thought I saw there. That day in the woods above the Yuba I learned that I hadn't been mistaken. I want a partner, and you 're the man for the business. By this time you know what I 'm driving at. I 'm a leveler — take from the rich, and give to the poor — beginning at home. I trust you. If you do not decide to join hands with me, why — you could stay here, and no one would ever know. But, friend, I trust you. Join with me or not, you leave here with my secret, and I do not think you will squeal on me. I hope we 'll yoke up, and make a good team of it."

Now, everything had been uncovered, and I knew that I was face to face with a self-confessed robber, who wished me to enter into a partnership with him in his criminal business. I did not know whether to feel flattered by his estimate of me, or disgusted that I should have made this bandit take me for good material for his evil deeds. However it might seem to me later, at the moment I could not harden myself toward him as my conscience and home training should prompt me. I turned to him — kindly, yes, that's the word, "kindly," and rising, shook my head as though turning aside from his offer, as I might from any ordinary one that had been made to me in an ordinary manner.

"No," I said, "I'll stick with the company. It may not be so bad as you think. I came here for that, and if it's only another failure — well, never mind — it's all in a life time, you know."

I walked with him over the pass, and back toward the miners' hotel, but Buck continued on in another direction. Perhaps I should have reported him to the owners of the mines. Without doubt I should have done so. But I did not repeat that experience to anyone for some time, and I cannot for the life of me explain why I did not give this man up to justice.

Chapter XV

THE YUBA MINING COMPANY

To judge from appearances, the company with which I was associated was doing a fair paying business. We were working on a river-bed claim, boasting a head and tail dam, with overflow box to convey the rising water above, across the basin, and over the tail dam, to the lower flow of the river below. The basin was pumped out by two bucket pumps, each throwing out an eight by sixteen-inch stream of water, worked by an over-shot wheel. In the basin bottom were all kinds of gear, from rifle boxes to tins for washing and cleansing gold.

I had not invested heavily in the stock of the company, but I had some shares, my principal reason for not having more, being lack of funds wherewith to purchase them. I was acting both as carpenter and bookkeeper — a single entry pass-book holding the debit and credit accounts, did not interfere with my daily duties as carpenter, nor did it enlighten me as to the true financial condition of the company.

I worked on with the others for, perhaps, three or four weeks, when a most unexpected catastrophe occurred, and with this was wiped out all question of the quality of the claim upon which the company had staked its all.

One morning we came to the river-bank, and there found a great upheaval, and a wild condition of things, caused by the rising of the river during the night. The waters had risen fifty feet! Machinery and dams were entirely swept away — all was as level and bare as though they had never existed! Not a vestige remained of the gear and machinery, that had been erected in this wilderness, at such an expense of energy and muscle, with no return to show for it all. It was a tragedy impossible to estimate to those deeply interested in the claim. It had now become to me the same old story of disappointment, and did not touch me so keenly; perhaps I had rather expected some disaster, and so took the real development of the event as a huge joke.

We were a set of forlorn looking individuals, without funds to start again. We even had succeeded in turning a branch of the Yuba, but the melting snow from the mountains, and heavy rains, blasted the enterprise, took almost our last penny, and killed all hope of getting gold when it seemed within our reach. We all took the occurrence philosophically with the exception of one poor fellow, who was much older than the rest of us. He had lost everything, and with his money he had lost his courage to start again. The boys were already making fresh plans, and dreaming of brighter fields ahead, but this man refused to leave the scene of the disaster, and the last view I had of him, he stood near the bank of the river watching the raging stream thunder down onto the rapids below. Thus ended the existence of the Yuba Mining Company.

Several mornings later a group of the fellows sat together making plans for the future, when a number of men in miners' rig rushed past our camp, all in great excitement. They waved to us in the direction from which

they had come. We thought new diggings had been discovered, and our courage rose, for it takes but little to
arouse the confidence, and hope of the miner. I hastened
to one of the excited men, keeping in step with him as he
hurried onward. The last disappointment to find the
color, never quenches the expectation that gold is waiting
at the next turn to be discovered.

"Where is it?" still beside him.

"Half a mile below — Barton's Bar — Cholera —
Thirty men dead out of a hundred!"

And the troubled miner rushed onward, followed by
many others all headed up the river to French Corral.
The men with whom I had now been associated for several
months decided to remain in the present camp to await
developments. It would seem — if cholera were epidemic
— as safe here where it had not made its appearance, as
in a new section where these men who had been exposed
to the disease might carry it. So here we stayed, with but
one case, and that was the last we heard or thought of
cholera.

Believing this section to be exhausted as far as gold
offered, I had decided to move on into fresh fields, when
an old Newburyport friend, Captain Leonard Noyes, a
near neighbor of mine at home, dropped in upon us one
evening. He had been away from home for a number of
years, acting as captain of a lake steamer, but had at last
caught the gold fever and found his way to California.

Captain Noyes persuaded me to change my mind, and
instead of seeking new diggings, to remain here and form
another company. This I did, and the new company was

formed with the Captain as president (we insisted that he should fill the position of president, as he was older, very able and efficient) and nine of the members of the extinct Yuba Mining Company. Newly equipped and confident of success this time (the elastic quality of the miner's faith to sometime find gold is forever on the rebound), we started again, not over a gunshot back from our old river-bed claim. We sank shafts, — coyoting, drifting in and on every promising appearing spot. Long lines of sluice, and rifle boxes were constructed, pipes and gauge ways were laid for water. In the surrounding territory we examined every rock or soil, that offered the slightest prospect of gold. All the effort was unsuccessful, and in the end we abandoned the whole scheme as a failure !

Chapter XVI

INDIANS ON THE WARPATH

It is my opinion that no more determined men ever organized, or more persistently tried to find gold than this company headed by Captain Noyes — but, the gold was not there to be found — or they would have had it! Now, there was no other alternative but to disband. We had been together for two months without even bearing a name as an organized body, but, although representing many callings, professors, mechanics, sailors, salesmen and traders, yet, we were a happy family. Many an evening after work there were heated discussions between our salt-water, and fresh-water members — two had never sailed on salt-water and two had never sailed on fresh. Two had sailed on the sea, and two only on the lakes.

Gathered around a brisk log fire, — if the evening was cold, as they frequently were in California — with the shadows of the great hills rising like dim buttresses around us, sometimes with a bright moon flinging the heavy bulk of the mountains black against the sky, there our sailors gathered and talked of the sea or of the great lakes. What had these towering peaks to do with the sea? We drew in around the "tars" and listened as the argument waxed warmer. An approving laugh sometimes cut into the discussion, but if they disagreed there was a jovial understanding to disagree in all good humor, and not with bad blood.

"But," held forth a "salt," "You can never bring the cabin and the forec'stle together! No, sir! No ship is safe without two ends — the after end for authority and the forward one for submission. It's a case of no rule or all rule. Just take the case of the 'Julia Belle.' If there had been a firm hand aft from the beginning of that voyage, do yer think Capt. Jones would have nearly starved on that island, while his mate brought the brig in with a mutinous crew. No, sir! That mate would have been in irons, with half the crew if need be, and at first sign of disobedience. You just take that from me."

A fresh log on the fire startled the shadows in the background over against the side of the mountain, but the young "freshie" saw only the blue of his lake, and the conditions on his ship as he had found them there.

"There you are!" said the freshie, "What you say only goes to prove what I 'm telling you. Sailors are men, and as such they should mix with the officers. The forward end of a ship is just as respectable as the after end. The 'Julia Belle' was just an exception — there are weak men everywhere, you see them mining, and you see them sailing or commanding a ship. More freedom, and less restraint, say I!"

And so the evening wore on, with neither convinced that his arguments were unsound; — both firm in the deeply rooted prejudices of time and custom.

The members of this unnamed company were all intelligent, and were a jovial set of fellows, and we disliked the thought of separating. We finally disbanded, each following a new enterprise — the group melting away, as it were, and again becoming individual units.

While looking around for new fields to conquer, I met a man who was taking a company on to the Kamath Diggings, in northern California. He had a good number of men and mules with him, while the company was well equipped with tools of many kinds, besides all necessities for the expedition. Each man was provided with a mule, and these animals were used to convey the mining gear. I thought this might be a good opportunity to get into something more fortunate than my other attempts had so far proved. I presented myself to the leader, and was promptly engaged to accompany him. And shortly I found myself mounted on a wiry, self-opinionated little beast, who apparently had small faith in his rider's judgment, and who proceeded to show his lack of respect by using his own diabolical methods. However, I managed to retain my *hold* upon his back.

The leader of the party, called by the men Captain Marx, was a Jew, and a stranger in this part of the country. I was soon a member of this new organization bound for entirely fresh claims, with, however, the same object and motive as before spurring me on. Our cavalcade moved rather slowly forward, until we came to the Sacramento River (not far from where Shasta now stands) — after still further delay in fording the river, for the mules ferried us across, we shortly arrived at the camping site of the company. Here I had my first opportunity to learn any definite information about Captain Marx our leader. It proved that he was not a miner, but rather was engaged in the business of trading. In company with one other man he owned large ranches, several mining claims, was proprietor of a store stocked with miners' tools of all descriptions, and groceries, owned many horses and mules, and besides all this, ran large pack-trains.

The company had been prospecting for several days, when an obstacle that I had not met before presented itself. The word reached camp that unfriendly Indians were on the warpath. This rumor was followed closely by an unmistakable challenge. A mule dashed past us with several arrows deeply imbedded in his rump. An old trader informed us that undoubtedly this meant only one thing, and that was war! We quickly held an impromptu council among ourselves, and decided that we must get out, and that it must be done as promptly as possible. Another company was formed with all haste, and headed for the most direct route to the coast. On the way our path lay over Salmon Mountain, and here we camped for the night, for there was little to be feared from the Indians in this location.

The temperature at this altitude was bitter cold; so cold that the water froze in our cans near at hand. But rolled in blankets, within the range of warmth from a roaring log fire, although the air tingled as in December, we did not mind it. In the valley below the weather was warm for it was summer, and we soon realized the difference in descending the mountain in the morning.

Urging our mules for a few days longer our little company reached Trinidad, a small station on the coast. The town consisted of a saw-mill, and a small cluster of houses. At the pier lay a lumber vessel, ready to take on her cargo. Here I obtained work, with several others, as a handler, and when the vessel was loaded took passage on her for San Francisco.

I now had traveled the rounds: from 'Frisco to the American River, then by way of Shasta to the coast. Now, again for 'Frisco which will connect the two lines, and also end a tramp that boasts more miles than nuggets.

Chapter XVII

THE SOLITARY GRAVE

AFTER months of strenuous but unsuccessful effort in the mines I found myself back in San Francisco. My pockets were empty as they had been following each of my former mining ventures, and while a certain discouragement lurked near my heart, yet a bravado, perhaps, prevented any acknowledgement of the fact even to myself. The actual expense of living was still a grave consideration in San Francisco, and the simple necessities of life forced one to be "up and doing."

However, I had always been able to secure some occupation wherewith to meet my immediate needs, and to put something by for a later-day journey into the mines. Never a time came when the motive for remaining on the coast was not prompted by the hope that sometime I should be successful in discovering gold.

With the thought that "here I am again back at the beginning," I went over the well-known grounds in search of whatever I might turn my hands to do, and shortly found it in driving piles.

I worked at pile-driving, furnishing the legs and feet for "Frisco's" wharves and buildings for three or four months. Here came the great firs of Oregon, and here many of the kings of those lordly forests humbly supported the caps of the city's wharves, or dug deep into the sand to hold up the new and more substantial structures that were fast being built. Among these buildings we drove the pile foundations for the new custom house.

After four months of excellent business our orders became fewer and fewer, until the firm considered it wisest to dissolve. Various reasons were given to account for this falling off in the erection of the city buildings. Some said speculators had cornered the stock, and stopped the trade; others that the bitterness between Spanish title-holders, squatters, and Mexican claimants to the land, must first be decided before sufficient confidence could be established to secure rightful titles.

With the unsettled condition of trade as a very convincing excuse, and a reassuring plumpness to my purse, my thoughts again turned in the direction of the mines. At this favourable moment what was my surprise and satisfaction to meet two old friends, Capt. Alexander Coffin and Joseph Tucker! Always in starting upon my mining ventures I readily found congenial companions to share the enterprises, and make the trips into the mines with me, and this social part of the adventures was ever, (to me) of very important concern, for a disagreeable partner could easily make conditions in the rugged life unbearable.

From Capt. Coffin and Mr. Tucker I learned that gold had been discovered in or near Tuolamnie. As this was in the southern section of California, it was necessary to take the night boat up the very crooked San Joaquin River.

Quickly deciding to enter into a partnership, we purchased an outfit, and secured passage on the river steamboat, a very poor, dilapidated old craft, for the following night.

The San Joaquin is, I believe, the most crooked river in the world. It coils between its banks as sinuously as a snake, and the poor old steamer when not sticking to the channel was sticking in the mud of its banks. When finally freed from the muddy hold, and again in the channel, it went thrashing its way through acres of wild oats fringing the shores, that brushed rasping sprays against our faces, and rendered life on the San Joaquin active if not peaceful and tranquil.

At last, after many drawbacks, we landed in Stockton, and found the place to be one where considerable business was carried on. From here we laid our course toward Sonora. Capt. Coffin and I were strangers to this part of the country, but Tucker had often traveled over these very trails; he acted as our guide, and told us all the history and legends of this part of southern California.

We entered upon a trail that lay for the greater distance over smooth level stretches. But gradually as we continued, our path became rougher, and more and more broken as we neared the mountains. Our guide brightened the way with stories of the many interesting scenes through which we were passing; so pleasantly did he entertain us that we forgot to be weary, and when at last we came to the journey's end, it was with regret that it had come to a close.

[The author took up the narrative of the trip to the mines of southern California upon arriving at Murphy's Camp. He noted many of the experiences along the rough trail, and recorded those that impressed him most.]

On the afternoon of the second day after leaving Stockton, we were walking over long wastes of barren prairie, the trail lying through rough, scrubby vegetation covering the sandy land for miles in all directions, when far ahead, just dimly seen in the distance rose something that appeared to us like the outlines of a low building.   Strange, we thought to see a house in the midst of this desert!

As the path shortened between us and the small object it did not resemble the framework of a house, so much as it did that of a tiny fortress,—low, and flat, and block-like it faced us. Capt. Coffin turned to me as we trudged onward and said,

"What do you make of it?"

"It's a mystery, certainly! who could have built a house in this desolate place?" I answered.

At this moment Tucker joined us, and overhearing our conversation said,

"Wait awhile. When we reach the spot I'll tell you all about it, for it has a history, and not a pleasant one either."

We quickened our steps as our curiosity was now fully aroused. As we drew nearer the structure, it did not look either like a house or fortress, but laid low and white — we could distinctly make out the color — within the heart of the great rolling prairie.

A half mile further, and we discovered the mystery! — a simple white fence enclosing a simple mound of earth! A grave in the lonely heart of the desert. A lonely enough resting-place!

"This grave," said Tucker as we circled the spot, and peered between the rude laths forming the fencing, "is that of a murdered miner. Just in the center where the mound is, his body was found. He had been shot in the back. That 's enough, isn't it, to tell the story? — in the *back*. He left Stockton with a pile of gold-dust. He 'd been lucky the season before, and had gone into town for fresh supplies. There he met a stranger, pleasant and agreeable, and bound in his direction. They left in each others' company — that was' told afterwards, — both headed for the mines in the mountains. Nothing definite was ever really known, but it all points to the one thing — he 'd told the fine stranger about his gold dust — well, anyway, nothing more was heard from either of them, until this body was found here, shot in the back." We were listening closely to Tucker's story.

"Did they ever find the murderer?" asked Coffin.

"No," answered Tucker, "He just vanished. It was too late when they found the body to do anything about it."

Leaving the small plot, with its solitary occupant there alone, we continued along the trail, but a gloom I could not get rid of clung to me for some time afterwards. The picture of that deserted and nameless grave haunted me. Relatives were waiting for him somewhere — waiting for the word that never came. And they would continue to wait — and, never, never would know!

We three fellows walked onward in silence, until Coffin broke it with,

"Thank God the poor wretch found some one kind enough to dig him a grave, and place his body in its last resting-place. And he also had the grace to paint the rough boards of the fence."

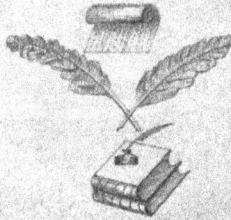

REPRODUCTION OF ENTRIES IN RICHARD HALE'S
JOURNAL

Our thoughts were following the same path as the Captain's, but we made no answer.

"Yes," continued he, "and thank God for a soul free from murder! Think of this criminal with his blood-stained hands — wherever he goes he will carry the agony of his victim's last moments. He may never be brought to justice — but he cannot escape his conscience. The sight of his ill-gotten gold will only the more remind him of his crime."

In this mood we pursued our way on and slowly up to the higher grade of the mountains. Little arose to break the silence. Occasionally an eagle wheeled and soared in his solitary flight, or a mourning dove crooned plaintively from one of the few solitary trees.

Thus we walked on, until at last we came to Jamestown Plain. From the gloom of this dismal desert we entered one of earth's natural flower gardens. I have never seen anything to excell the beauty of the great plain of flowers rolling as the sea before a gentle breeze, each wave crested with blossoms of many hues. Among this wild garden of ravishing color, I recognized many varieties I was familiar with in the east, and many others I had never before seen, all growing as nature had planted them in glorious profusion. Knee-deep we waded through the billows of blossoms, while birds as glowing in plumage as the petals of the flower flitted about us, but no song, no clear, sweet bird-notes came from their dainty throats. This was all a picture to gratify the eye, the ear caught nothing that the gamut of color suggested, unless the continuous whispering of the flowers brushed by the wind tempted the ear to listen to their confession. I could only stand like one

> "With eye entranced,
> While sleeps the ear."

Tucker is ever matter-of-fact, and sees only the financial side of even the most beautiful things.

"There's money in this!" he exclaimed, all the while tramping down the waving beauties.

"The day will come, now mark my words, when these grounds will be a great paying institution. Better than gold-dust — shipping these seeds east! I have my method too. When the seeds are ripe, the birds, the first reapers, will have full stored crops, and will be fat and lazy, and easily caught. Then take out the crops, and dry them. When they are thoroughly dry, sew 'em up, and send the full crops to market. By this method the very best seeds will be secured, for the birds select only the largest and best, and reject the hollow and worthless ones."

Capt. Coffin and I hastened onward, loath to crush so much loveliness under our feet, but also wondering at a blindness that permitted only one object to be distinguished.

For hours we traveled across the kaleidoscopic prairie, then we laid our way to Sonora and from there continued our walk to Murphy's Camp. This mining camp is well up on the side of the hills that look down upon a narrow and nameless creek. The banks descend steeply, and the creek, a few feet in width, has a flat sandy shore. There was no need to build a cabin, for we came upon a deserted one of logs, on a level nook sheltered by the rise of the mountains, and it proved to be a very comfortable little home. Our cabin stood at a fair altitude above the plain, and from it there showed a panorama of lofty foothills, and soft green valleys, with the creek far below. The valley beneath us was so smoothly covered with tall grass, that it almost resembled a New England hayfield. Here were at least thirty or forty acres of beautiful grassland, planted by nature, and reaped only by herds of grazing deer. But we seldom saw the deer, for they made their visits by night, and departed before the occupants of the cabin so far above them, unwrapped their blankets. Yet, in stepping out of our small home upon the flat shelf of rock and stubbly grass, the early sun picking out, and bringing into sharp relief the crowns of the great hills, while it illumined the beauty of the valley, there within the deep grass of the plain, their tracks showed plainly enough where the shy creatures had been during the night, for the very imprints of their bodies, and their feet in the crumpled grass, told of the nightly visit. Our little company carried no weapons, of any sort, either as protection to ourselves, or with which to secure game.

Each day found us prospecting, digging and panning in every manner possible, but we met with no success worth mentioning. Finally we extended our efforts from our own claim by the creek, to the adjoining country — bars, flats, river beds, slides, crevices, alluvials, whatever favouring spot we happened upon, there we tried our luck, but with all our efforts we discovered little dust.

Chapter XVIII

IN THE DIRECTION OF CALLAO

LIVING for weeks so intimately as had the Captain, Joe and I, with small chance of seeing and speaking to any humans, we had had ample opportunity to know each other as perhaps few would know us during the rest of our natural lives. The Captain, as I have said before, was considerably older than Joe and I, and in our chats at night he "spun yarns" of his years as captain on a Liverpool liner; and yet the love of adventure, and the desire to make his fortune, had drawn him across the seas into the mines of southern California. As I saw and became more deeply acquainted with him, I found him to be a man of great strength of character, yet of much kindness of heart; ever ready to perform a good or kindly deed — ever ready to give an encouraging or cheering word; — his slogan in times of indecision "Two wrongs never make a right." He, very likely, as Captain of the liner, enacted the part of a stern and strict disciplinarian, but with us he shared an equal partnership — one of three miners. I shall never forget him, or his fatherly advice, for I confess to needing it in moments of rashness.

Joe Tucker, undoubtedly was by far the most experienced miner of the three; — there was no trail, bearing, or lay of mining land that he was not familiar with. He knew them as well as the streets of his native city, and he always acted as our guide. His endurance as a walker was remarkable, great distances over rough trails being easily covered by him in one day. But it was during our evenings together following the work of the day, when with comparative comfort in the cozy mountain home we talked intimately of former ventures and experiences since coming to the coast, that Joe confided to us his former success and his foolish and unwise losses. Three times he had found rich deposits, that had given him small fortunes; three successive times he had made poor investments, and lost everything, and so here he was, beginning again as at first.

Day after day when the sun penetrated the shadows of the creek, it found us starting forth with our mining tools, still confident that today gold would shine in our pans, but as day after day followed with no success, and week succeeded week with continued failure, — finally, our supplies getting low — we became convinced that the claim and the surrounding territory had been exhausted, and we must give it up as another disappointment!

Already some arrangements had been made for a move toward Stockton, when two men — miners who were prospecting with their tools — came past the camp, and learning that we were about to leave it, asked permission to try their luck in a small shaft that the evening before we had abandoned. They worked over the very spot we had left as worthless, and within an hour came to a little pocket just below the hole made by the last shovel-full thrown up the night before. Here they took out seven dollars in pure gold. Their success gave us fresh courage, and again we set to work on the claim. For several days

we went at it with a will, but try as we might no gold rewarded our efforts, and as the stores were becoming too
low to remain any longer without new supplies, a council
was called, with the decision that Stockton must be our
objective, and that at once.

All things being ready for a start the night before, — the
sun had not yet risen, when carrying our packs, we began
the forty-mile walk that would bring us to a comfortable
shelter — so said Tucker — for the night. Our little home,
on the steep hillside had grown dear to each of us, and as
we gave a final look through the dusk of the morning to
the objects so familiar, the shadowy mountains over beyond the creek, the plain lying dim and misty in the deeper
shadows, the steep rough path we had traveled down to
the deep still water, it was with regret that we turned
away from it all, and started on the straightest and
shortest cut to Stockton.

Forty miles of steady tramping on the trail brought us
by nightfall to very comfortable shelter, which we deeply
appreciated, and very much needed, for the day had been
a hard one. The cabin was small, but the occupants
showed a kindly and hospitable spirit, furnishing us with
a good supper, and bunks and blankets for the night. I
slept so soundly that it seemed I had scarcely been asleep,
when we were called for breakfast, as an early start was
advisable to continue the remaining walk of twenty-five
miles to Stockton.

The twenty-five miles quickly disappeared, and again
we were in Stockton. As there were several hours to while
away before our departure, I had a pleasant call on the

Mayor of the town. He was a man by the name of Fowler, who had been a former resident of Newburyport. He impressed me very favorably, and seemed a man of considerable ability with pleasant, agreeable manners. Following an hour in his office, I joined my two companions, and shortly we were on the night boat on the way to 'Frisco, arriving at the city in the early morning. Here Capt. Alexander Coffin, of Hudson, N. Y., and Joseph Tucker of Newburyport and myself parted, and with moistened eyes we bade each other goodby. The hardships and disappointments had but cemented our friendship until we had become like one family, and it was with deep regret that I bade the Captain and Joe farewell as they went on into the mountains still in quest of gold.

[Capt. Coffin never returned from this venture into the mines. The author of the journal some years later met Mr. Tucker after he had returned to his home in Newburyport. From him he learned of the death of the Captain, and also some of the painful details. Joseph Tucker proved a faithful friend and attendant, caring for his friend until the end.]

As on numerous other occasions, I now found myself in San Francisco, pursuing the same all-important object — that of securing the wherewithal to sustain life. For several weeks it seemed rather a difficult problem, and I tried my hand at most anything and everything, including lightering, painting, carpentering, with a little cooking thrown in during an absence of anything else to do. Matters settled down finally, with a steady increase to my income, but I found that I had become a product of the times, and the place. Conditions here could not be judged by the old conservative New England standards.

Nothing in San Francisco was stationary — everything and everybody was in constant motion — on the wing! The desire to move swept through the air, clutching all within the radius of its circle. Ever there was the money status — will it pay? will it pay? There were but two answers to this question — Yes — No — and in this manner right and wrong were balanced. In the east the Yankee was walled about by forms, creeds and conventions. His own name, and the names of his sires must be public property, and their records must be spotless. He shared his grandsire's virtues, or his vices — judged by public opinion. Often he was raised to a pinnacle by the act of some ancestor, or was drawn to disgrace in the same manner. But here there were no questions asked about pedigree. "Can he fill the position? If he can, well and good, if not — let us have one who can fill it." It was an easy matter to make a Yankee into a Californian, but no easy matter to make him back again. From the man with many opinions as to personal values, as he was in the east — on the Pacific coast he learned to have but two estimates "be a man, or be made one."

It would not be true to say that crime did not exist, for often San Francisco was the refuge of the outlaw, but on the whole I believe conditions made for higher manhood in the end. The "Vigilanters" were a law unto themselves, ferreting out criminals, and meting out punishments severe and sudden. However that may have been, the safety of the people called for radical means whereby to keep crime in check. The sudden clang of the bell! Who did not know what its ringing foretold? "Death!"

"Death!" it generally pealed to the waiting listeners, while a body dangled from the derricks of the Sand Lot, the Plaza or Russian Hill. But the prompt and extreme measures of the "Vigilanters" were breaking up the rule of the outlaw, and bringing in a better and safer order of things.

The city seemed crowded with new people, they swarmed the streets, and filled every available place. The rainy season loomed at hand and brought with its downpour anything but comfortable conditions. During one of my walks at this time I came upon Capt. Rogers of Newburyport, then captain of the ship *Beatrice*. Our meeting was a surprise to us both. Although many from our home city had caught the lust for gold and were seeking it in California, the Captain was not here for that purpose, but as commander of a ship about to sail for Callao. I decided to make the run down with him. The rainy season over — so I argued to myself — a passage back to San Francisco could easily be obtained, while a disagreeable California winter could thus be avoided.

With this thought in mind, I made a round of the town and the old friends, for now I had been over three years on the Pacific coast, and felt myself to be a seasoned Californian. My walk included the site of our first small home on Telegraph Hill, but as I stood looking off over the city, and out over the beautiful bay, little reminded me of that earlier time, save the curve of the shore, and even that had been altered by the many wharves and piers reaching out into its waters. Several substantial buildings, (the custom house among them) rose up from the level of the town below me. I was about to return to my lodgings in the city, when a friend overtook me, and during our talk told of the death by fever of David Pingree, our cook on the *Gen. Worth,* also of the death of George Stockman, a passenger on the *Gen. Worth,* the latter had been employed as engineer on the steamer *Eagle,* and when it had been blown up a few weeks before he had been killed with several others.

This was all sad news, and I was very sorry to hear it. I had now fully made up my mind to sail with Capt. Rogers, and after attending to what business seemed necessary in order to leave the city, I packed my belongings and turned my face in the direction of Callao.

Chapter XIX

THE BURIED CITY

O<small>N</small> September 9th, 1853, I boarded the ship *Beatrice* and sailed from San Francisco to Callao, Peru, South America. As I stood on deck under the spread of sail for the first time since passing through the Golden Gates three years before, I fully expected to return at the close of the wet season; and my departure would have been less casual had I known that with the sailing of the *Beatrice* I bade goodby forever to my associates and associations in California.

Our passage to Callao proved most harmonious, in fact everything inboard and out moved so smoothly that little occurred worth mentioning. Our ship was one to be proud of — our captain capable and kind, — our officers efficient — the elements genial and favoring. However, one incident arose to cause considerable commotion during the run down.

The ship's cook could not escape notice. He was a series of contradictions — the most amusing medley of opposing qualities imaginable. He had the face of a great overgrown boy — round eyed, with two or three curves to his double chin, while the white crest of hair confessed that he was well along in years. His trousers usually stopped at his knees, disclosing immense round calves, and his entire figure gave the impression of an inflated boy, for he undoubtedly weighed more than two hundred pounds, while

123

all his motions were quick, and reminded one of a child.
He would begin a sentence in deep masculine voice, but
finish it an octave higher. Suddenly while talking to a
man, one found himself without warning holding conversation with a child or woman, — the cook's voice had
leaped into the falsetto at a bound, and from the man he
at once had turned into an immense boy.

He furnished considerable amusement for those on
board ship and many excuses were found to stop near the
galley and ask him some question, or try to engage him in
conversation. He had a most ungovernable temper, and
it found vent upon captain or cabin boy — whichever
came upon him in his moments of anger.

I was aft one morning when a great commotion arose in
the vicinity of the galley — oaths in a man's deep voice
were followed by the unmistakable cries of a woman.
There were no women aboard, and I immediately thought,
"A woman stow-away! Where has she hidden herself
all this time!"

Being busy and not able to go at once to the scene of
the outcry, I listened to the apparent tragic drama of an
enraged man, forcing a shrieking female from her hiding-
place. I hastened to the galley as quickly as possible, for
one could not but feel sympathy with a woman, who had,
for some purpose, best known to herself, secreted herself
in some uncomfortable place on board the ship, hoping to
remain undiscovered until the vessel touched port.

Near the galley a number of the passengers and crew
had gathered, while in their midst stood the cook, gesticu-
lating wildly, and with each successive gesture landing a

fresh article of his bedding or baggage among his audience. At the same time a bull-like bellow roared out all manner of cursings, always terminated by the falsetto of a woman's shriek. Well, all anyone could do was simply to hold on to his own sides and laugh, for the whole exhibition displayed the temper of an enraged child, with the profane language of a bad sailor, and there was no way to pacify or quiet him, until like a bad child he had worn himself out.

Finally the captain heard the disturbance, and we saw him coming toward the galley, and made a passage for him. The cook saw him, too, but the captain had no quieting effect upon his rage — it only added fuel to the fire.

"Turn the d——n old hulk — turn her, I say — Put me ashore — (bass) — put me ashore — (soprano) — D'yer hear — (bass) — d'yer hear — (soprano) —r-r-r-r whoaw"—ranging from bass to soprano, while he accented the range of his voice by throwing pieces of his garments wherever they might land, one hitting the captain full in the face.

The captain had him put in irons, but even then he was not silenced, until threatened with the gag, but the fear of that subdued him. He broke into tears of rage like a bad and naughty child, and was soon asleep upon the deck. The crew laughingly replaced his dunnage, and he soon after revived sufficiently to prepare a good dinner. We never learned the cause of the cook's rage. Perhaps he had been imbibing too freely — we never learned, and the affair was soon forgotten.

The incident of the cook supplied the only excitement of the voyage. The run down to Callao glided by with such smoothness that week followed week in the same delightful way, and the voyage really had ended before we realized the length of the trip of nearly two months.

Occasionally a sail came within speaking distance, or we sighted a school of whales spouting between the ship and the horizon. At times the ship pushed through thousands of porpoises and blackfish — thus everything passed serenely until on November 4th the island of San Lorenzo was sighted near the entrance of Callao Bay. After several tackings to take advantage of a light and almost head wind, the *Beatrice* reached the grounds for anchoring, and our voyage of fifty-five days from San Francisco came to an end.

Callao is the seaport of Lima, and as we viewed it from the deck, with its great grim fortress facing the bay, we judged it to be a good-sized city. In the harbor at anchor were perhaps three hundred and fifty sail, all bound for the Chincha Islands to get cargoes of guano, and afterwards we learned that all the vessels were headed eastward. My only thought, when reaching Callao, was to return to San Franciso as soon as possible, for at the end of the return voyage, the rainy season would be well over, and again I could make a visit to the mines. Not a ship in the harbor was northward bound, and the only alternatives were a trip to the Chinchas, or one by way of the Cape home. I decided in favor of the Chinchas, and soon agreed to ship as carpenter on the ship *Pauline*, of Bath, Maine, for on the return, a vessel going to San Francisco might in the meantime have come into the port of Callao.

The *Pauline* was not to sail for the Chinchas for several days, and during that time I decided to explore the city of Callao, and Lima, the capital of Peru since the time of Pizarro. Eagerly, I had always read any story referring to that wonderful country of the Incas, with its remarkable, and picturesque civilization in existence so many hundreds of years ago, and now that I found myself at the very door of a land, that had yielded gold and silver to fill Spanish galleons innumerable, I could scarcely restrain an impulse to rush ashore, and view a place filled with so much that was interesting.

The following morning we landed, and after finding no northern bound ship — as I have before noted — I began my tour of exploration around Callao. During the search for passage to San Francisco I met a young man, a native of Callao, who could speak and understand some English, while I could speak and understand a little Spanish. In this manner we got on very well, and he kindly offered to take me over the city, and show me the places I most wished to see. In some vague way previously I had heard of the great earthquake of 1746, but had never, and have never since, read any account of the results of this terrible calamity. At the time of the earthquake a great tidal wave flooded the city, burying it below a newly-made bay, extending far inland.

My new acquaintance first pointed to the Island of San Lorenzo, that with the neighboring island of Fronton protect the harbor.

"That island," he said, speaking in very broken English, with an occasional word in Spanish, "is the island of

San Lorenzo." He waved his hand toward the central peak towering to a height of fully a thousand feet. "We have a good story of the island and the earthquake. San Lorenzo was not there until it rose up — up from the bottom of the sea. A fisherman, at the time of the earthquake was sitting upon the small spot of land where you now see the top of the mountain. He was fishing in the bay. All in a moment he found himself a thousand feet in the air, while around him were sounds of rushing waters, and where there had been the solid land, was raging water, and where there had been water, was dry earth, but the fisherman remained on the mountain unharmed — the only person in all the city to escape the tidal wave and the earthquake! And they made him *Saint* Lorenzo, for his name was Lorenzo. It is more than legend," as I questioned him regarding the truth of the story — "the story is a true one, for, come, I will show you Saint Lorenzo's grave."

And my new acquaintance showed me a grave on which was carved the name "San Lorenzo." Perhaps the story was true, for from others I heard the same tale, with the added fact that the future saint hurried down the mountain unharmed, and succeeded in gaining a place of safety. All his family, and the entire city had been destroyed, and to the church it seemed a direct intervention of Providence, and he was canonized as a Saint. I turned and looked with more interest at the mountainous island, stretching for four miles along the entrance to the bay, — long and high and slender.

My guide led me from one marvel of nature's tragic

HUMMING BIRD

TITMOUSE

BLUE JAY

LAND BIRDS SKETCHED BY RICHARD HALE

work to another. We walked along a low promontory or raised reef, composed of flat stones. For half a mile or more the rough path trailed on, out into the bay, until the young man paused and pointed downward.

"See! the buried city of Callao!" The sight was weird and awful in the extreme. Just in front of us the water seemed shoal, and dashed wildly over what appeared to be a submerged reef.

"Come here — look!"

Looking into clearer and smoother depths I could plainly see vaults, and unroofed walls, with floors thickly strewn with what looked like human bones. These walls varied in height, but they extended out into the bay for a considerable distance, some of the higher points broke through the surface of the water, which for more than a hundred years had battered them in vain. The sensation as I stood on that narrow foothold composed of the very remnants of the demolished city perhaps, was grewsome and filled with horror. I thought of that awful moment when midst seething earth and flooding wave, thousands of people met their death! As we retraced our steps, my guide pointed to a spot where it was believed the golden gates of the great cathedral lay buried.

"The gates of the cathedral are buried beneath," he said, indicating a certain spot well under water. "The punishment is death to exhume them. The good Lord took them for His own special purpose, and in His own good time will restore them. Several have been shot for mining for them."

Somewhat farther back, by a wave of his hand he

called my attention to what looked like the masts of a fore-and-aft vessel. They were well back from the waters of the bay, and about half buried under thick grass-sod.

"At the time of the earthquake this vessel was lying at anchor. The bay was then dry land, and this whole level place, and nearly all the island of San Lorenzo were covered with water."

He led on until the apparent results of the terrible cataclysm were lost in the rise of the new Callao. As I looked back, there rose the masts, tall, and straight, and well-preserved, above their buried hulk — there they stood, and will stand without doubt for years to come, for the people are superstitious, many believing it to have been the work of God, and that He does not wish His work disturbed.

In our walk through new Callao we came upon a long procession of people, they were marching with upturned faces, some with their hands extended, and were chanting, as though appealing to a higher power to protect them from some evil. Again and again they repeated their refrain, some with pale and tear-stained faces.

"What does this mean?" I demanded of my acquaintance in some excitement.

"The yellow fever has made its appearance," he answered, "They are praying to be spared, or that a member of their family may be spared, or that a friend may not be smitten, or may recover."

I had followed the procession with such interest that I had not noticed where my steps were leading me, until without warning my hat was suddenly removed by a bay-

onet in the hands of an officer. I was about to show considerable indignation at such an insult, for so I deemed it,
when my friend quickly drew me aside.

"We were on holy ground," he whispered. "Did you not
see the body they were just carrying past us. You were in
luck that they did not remove your head instead of your
hat. Think yourself fortunate to be at the mercy of a
good fellow."

This seemed a fair explanation, and at once I turned and
nodded as though asking the officer's pardon, he replied
with a low and graceful bow, while we continued toward
the wharf with the ringing plaint of the chanters still in
our ears. Here I said goodby to my new-made friend, and
never saw him afterwards. I cannot vouch for the truth
of the legends, for undoubtedly in so terrible a time, fact
and fancy may have commingled, but with my own eyes
I saw the walls of sunken Callao lying beneath the waters
of the bay, and the masts of the sunken vessel breaking
the sod of a firmly growing grass-plot.

Chapter XX

THE REALM OF THE INCAS

In the morning in company with a friend from New-buryport whom I had met in Callao, we started out to see the city of Lima — historical, romantic city of ancient Spanish viceroys — of Pizarro the all-conquering hero — Pizarro the picturesque Spaniard, who with a few hundred followers had invaded and subdued the land of the mighty Incas. Here in Lima he had first set up the seat of government for his country, and with galleons filled with plundered gold and silver he had enriched the coffers of Spain. But it was as Pizarro the bold adventurer, the intrepid discoverer, I had always pictured him.

In a small English box car we rode over the rails for seven or eight miles in the direction of the city. At the end of that distance, rising thick and high before us loomed the walls surrounding Lima — scarred, and ancient, and grim they enclosed the capital. We left the car and entered through one of the heavy gates, here we were pestered by self-appointed guides begging us for permission to show us the sights of interest. These guides are little less than beggars, for on the slightest pretext they extend a begging hand, piteously asking for a real.

As we walked through the streets an atmosphere of age, yet an age that still held great strength in its sinews, pervaded everything about us. Most of the streets were straight, and many of them converged toward a great

square we saw in the distance. The blank walls of the
houses were windowless, with a few exceptions, while a
great door opened directly onto the roadway. Through
the door a passageway led into an inner court or patio,
around which the house was built. Down the middle of
the streets, flowed small streams of water used as open
drains, and on the sides of these drains stood great
turkey-buzzards, black, wide-winged creatures, ever on
the watch for a continuous carrion dinner.

On we walked until we came to a large stone bridge
crossing the River Rimac. The bridge arched the river
with a splendid curve of masonry, but like all other
things in the city of Lima, its stones were browned and
seamed with the course of the years. As we stood looking
at the structure, with the river cutting through and separating the city, our guide, who knew a few broken words
of English, eagerly waved his hand in the direction of the
bridge and cried,

"Ah — ah — ver — ver — builded — viceroy — Montes
Claras — 1613 hunderd year — presenta real."

We gave him the real, and gazing at the agonized expression of his swarthy countenance, and the anxiety with
which he watched the drop of the small coin into his out-
stretched palm, we judged he must be suffering great
distress — either pain or poverty, or both.

His information we interpreted thus: — The old stone
bridge had been erected in the year 1613, under the vice-
royship of the duke Montes Claras. Everywhere in the
city one came face to face with the early years of Spanish
rule.

Our guide hurried across the bridge into the suburb of San Lazaro. Here we felt the cooling shade from double rows of graceful willow trees, growing straight and sturdy under their fluttering foliage. These trees lined a fine avenue along the banks of the river, that led on to large buildings we could see in the distance.

"Do know what that structure is?" we asked our guide.

"Si, si, Signor — ver fine — gran'! — bull fight! — zee bull fight! — zee Viceroy Don Manuel Amat — 1770 hundred year — presenta real."

We eased his distress by placing the coin into his extended hand. How could we do otherwise, when we saw what instant relief this small bit of silver afforded him.

Within the big enclosure in the distance, bull fights had gratified the love of excitement of the natives since the year 1770, and it had been builded by the Viceroy Don Manuel Amat — so we interpreted the broken words of the guide.

Continuing our walk he next pointed out a quaint roof-less building, vast in extent, with box doors opening onto a gallery in the open air. This called into play all the dramatic fire of his excitable make-up.

"Ah — ah — ver — ver — opera — fine — fine. Ver — ver — opera — presenta real."

As the real seemed to be the most important point of interest always, and in every place, we now had it ready for him, and quickly passed it over.

Returning across the bridge we went along a broad avenue finally ending in the great square. Here indeed, the power of the viceroys, and their regal authority was revealed in the spaciousness of the vast public park; the cathedral, with its two high, square towers at either side, facing the square, and other public buildings, all telling of a past age, as they stood scarred and wrinkled under the blue of a tropic sky.

A fountain in the center of the square attracted us. Above the fountain a majestic figure in bronze looked out over the broad acres of the park.

For a moment we had forgotten the presence of our omnipresent guide. What could have diverted his attentions from his everlasting "real — presenta real?" However he returned to the attack with renewed vigor gained from the short respite.

"Ah — ah — Fame — zee   statue — Count   Salva tierra — 1653 hunderd year — presenta real."

Apparently in the brief silence the poor fellow had had time to realize more fully the awfulness of his condition, for his expression was far more wretched than ever before. We hastened to present the real, and immediately he recovered. However, we were not quite sure whether the Viceroy had posed for the statue, or whether it had been erected by him. Whichever way it might have been, the year 1653 had seen it placed in its present position above the fountain.

Our guide now entered the great cathedral. Vast and dim, vaulted and arched, it rose over the hidden chambers deep down within the earth, where they honey-combed subterranean depths. Aged was this old cathedral like everything else in this land of former greatness. In earlier days when the church was first erected, its high altar had shone with gold and silver taken from the treasures of the Incas, but we learned that the new republic had claimed these riches for its own.

We pointed toward the altar and asked our guide if at one time there had not been rich furnishings of precious metals there.

"Si, si Signor — ver great gold and seelver — Pizar-ro, he take zee gold and zee seelver from Cuzco" — the early seat of the Incas — "here, here — ver — rich" with a wave of his hand toward the altar, "all gone — no more — presenta real."

We knew what was coming, and had it ready, but for this long speech we feared his demand might be for more reals, but it was not, and during the entire time he was with us he never asked for more than one real, but he asked for that often.

Down into the corridors of the subterranean vaults we followed him, wondering at their mysterious secrets, for during hundreds of years they had crawled along in the dark beneath the ancient cathedral. Our guide stopped in front of a small chamber, its entrance guarded by iron bars. Between the bars we could see what looked like a little heap of dust lying upon a flat slab of stone. Here in great excitement he peered in through an opening, and directing our attention to the crumbling dust, with grimace and gesture cried,

"Ah — ah — ver! — ver! — zee great Piz-ar-ro — ver! — ver! Piz-ar-ro — presenta real."

This small pile of dust then, was all that remained to tell of Pizarro! The bold, the picturesque, the successful invader of the land of wonderful wealth in priceless metals — the realm of the Incas! We gazed, trying to believe that here, deep down in the vault beneath the church he had been instrumental in erecting perhaps, lay the dust of the old Conqueror. It might have been true, but of these stories to draw forth the real it was necessary to be wary, for the begging guides would show one anything one might ask to see.

We came up out of the dim and damp passages into the bright light of the early evening. We walked out through the park, and down the broad avenue that led to the gate of Lima. This we found closed for the night, and as we could not pass through it, we were obliged to remain in the city until the following morning. Pondering what to do and where to go, our guide plucked me by the sleeve, — for he was still with us! it seemed as if we could only get rid of him when the gate clanged behind him. — With a really splendid wave of his hand that included the circle of the wall surrounding the beautiful and interesting city of Lima he cried his last lay of the real.

"Si, si, signor — la Palata — zee Duke la Palata — zee wall builded — All! — ver — ver — zee wall — 1685 hunderd year — presenta real."

Without doubt "presenta Real" was the motto of his class, and never once did he forget it or omit it, and he followed his victims to the outer walls to be sure of the last real. But here we finally managed to leave him, and retraced our way to the hotel Bal-de-Ora, where we found fairly comfortable accommodations for the night.

Chapter XXI

GUANO AT THE CHINCHAS

THURSDAY, November 10, 1853. Boarded the ship *Pauline*, she weighed anchor, and before a soft tropical breeze we sailed from the Bay of Callao for the Chincha Islands, there to obtain a cargo of guano.

The days passed in the cities of Callao and Lima, notwithstanding the fact that yellow fever had broken out, and that many were ill, and some had already died with the terrible scourge — among the number our captain's brother — had been intensely interesting. During the time there I always contrasted the wild and pioneer life in Oregon and California, with the ancient Spanish settlements, and the earlier civilization of the Incas. The old buildings, the cathedrals, the substantial houses where families lived together after the fashion of the east, — though differing so greatly in speech, customs and dress, — with women and little children frequently to be seen, appealed to me strongly, after my years of isolation from all but the associations of rugged life on the coast.

The bow of the *Pauline* was pointed toward the Chinchas, and while I did not expect the visit at the islands to be pleasant, yet, it was the only way that offered a possible return to California.

On Monday, November 14th we sighted the Chincha Islands, and drawing nearer viewed them as they rose like beautiful gray-blue headlands out of a calm-lying blue

sea. The encircling waters seemed perfectly motionless, —
limpid, with deep shadows thrown from the pyramid-like
heights into clear depths beneath. There were three
islands, each rising out of the bay like a colossal, irregular
shaped ball, or like a great head resting upon gigantic
shoulders nearly hidden under the waters.

We finished our run down, and anchored in a sheltered
bay off the Middle island. Not since entering San Francisco harbor had I seen so many sail together. Hundreds
of vessels lay at anchor awaiting their turn to go under the
chute — a long box slide, through which the guano was
dumped from the island above into the hold of the ship.
Capt. Coburn — the captain of the *Pauline* — decided
not to go under the chute, but to load by boats, — a privilege granted him by the Peruvian government. As quickly
as the ballast was discharged from the ship's hold, its place
was filled by the guano. The government of Peru controlled everything connected with exporting the millions
of tons of the deposit, and received a vast revenue from its
trade in the fertilizer.

The attractive picture the Chinchas presented as we
approached them, resolved, as we drew nearer, into the
most barren place I had ever seen. Not a tree, a leaf, a
flower or a blade of grass grew on their repulsive wastes.
Before the islands were worked for the guano, it is said
that the birds that had nested there for countless ages,
when rising on the wing would darken the noonday sun,
and that the noise of the whirr of their wings was so
great that one could neither hear nor talk. At this same
period thousands upon thousands of immense sea-lions

lolled over the shelving shores, and millions of fish filled the waters at their base. That the bay still swarmed with fish I knew was true today, for I have seen schools of mackerel, their blue backs completely covering its surface. The sustenance of all this abounding life was purely animal — the larger preying upon the smaller, from the little hawk that alighted on our spars to devour his prey — himself later to furnish a meal for a more formidable foe — to the immense sea-lion breaking the face of the sea his mouth filled with fish in an easy catch.

The manner in which the guano was formed was wholly by the excrement and the bodies of animals and birds, accumulating throughout the years. The heguiro, the booby and the pelican were the chief workers. I did not see the process of manufacture going on, but I was informed that these grounds have been nesting colonies, — it was always to these islands, and a few other sections of the mainland, with a few other islands, that the birds came to raise their young. The nests were large, for the heguiro was much larger than a gull, and they were placed with the edges of the nests nearly touching, and these colonies extended over considerable extent, covering wide spaces of rock and shore. The nests were made by the male and female bird. As there was nothing for miles around from which to build the nests, they were constructed from the excrement of their bodies. In this manner the vast deposits of guano were finally made — tier over tier, or nest over nest.

For untold centuries this teeming life had swarmed around and on these islands. The deposits and the bodies had gradually raised the surface to such a great extent that millions of tons of guano was now exported by the government. Not only was the place most repulsive in odour and uncleanliness, but the manner in which the work was carried on was most inhuman. Coolies, and convicts from Peru, performed all the labour. The coolies were contract labourers, and were secured from China by agents who grossly misrepresent all the conditions here. They seemed to be under the worst kind of slavery, and under cruel masters.

I witnessed an exhibition of brutality such as I never wish to see again. One morning I had gone with the crew on the lighter to the island to secure a load of guano. The lighter was just touching the shore, when a shriek rang out from the cliff above us, and looking up in the direction of the cry, we saw a poor coolie rushing toward the brink. Behind him came his master, holding a many-tailed lash in his hands. On dashed the frightened Asiatic, and on dashed his master, until, before I could even cry out, the coolie reached the edge, and with one glance downward, plunged over upon the rocks two hundred feet below. The coolie knew he was plunging to his death, but preferred it to the lashes of his master's whip, and life under the awful conditions that existed on the islands.

The man with the whip on the cliff above, came to the edge of the overhang, and gave a casual glance below at the broken body lying on the rocks. But that was the only interest he displayed. He quickly disappeared, undoubtedly to continue his cruelties upon other unfortunates.

We hurried ashore, but the man was dead. His bruised body was lifted by his own countrymen, and placed within a weighted burlap bag, and then dropped into the bay. Not a day passed while we were at anchor off the islands, that we did not see the piteous upturned face of a dead coolie floating by. They preferred death to the terror of the place, and there was no chance of escape in any other way. Out of the thousands coming to the islands, drawn there by the false pretenses of the agents, a great number died by their own hand. — It was horrible to see these abandoned dead! A battlefield would have been less grewsome, I believe, for at some time the opposing sides had an equal chance to fight for life, but here there was only the taskmaster and his victim. The most shocking affairs happened around us. At one time a mangled body floated athwart the hawser, rising and falling as the motion of the ship tightened or slackened the cable, until our crew released it. Such sights were frightful to me: and the most difficult part of it all was one's helplessness to relieve the cruelties practiced upon the victims. The very air seemed poisoned and contaminated with the evil, and much trouble brewed in the great anchored fleet. Our own ship did not escape the virus.

Our cook, who also served as steward at the islands, was a peculiar mixture of Chinese with another strain that I never could quite make out. He had a sullen disposition and a desperate temper, and swaggered about the ship in a most independent manner. Mr. Bowers, — the mate taking the place of Capt. Coburn's brother who died of yellow fever at Callao, — the cook refused to accept as his superior officer, always responding to his orders with a sneer. Knowing the dispositions of the two men we all looked for trouble, and it was not long before it developed. Both had violent tempers, but the mate much to the surprise of everyone, had held his in check, until finding the cook persisted in insulting him, he felt forbearance had ceased to be a virtue. After a flagrant offense the mate responded by a stinging blow in the cook's face.

At the time the cook was in the galley preparing soup. He seized a ladle of hot soup and threw it on the bare head of the mate, then followed up the attack with a long wicked looking knife which he tried to plunge into Mr. Bowers' side. For a few minutes there was a sharp battle, until the mate finally overpowered him, and he was put in irons. There he remained till he made reassuring promises to be more civil, and never again to use soup or a knife for a similar purpose.

Our stay here has been dreary and depressing, and yet, as I am fully becoming convinced, most of our experiences are of value. I would not have foregone this one even, although there has been so little to enliven the weeks here.

One thing is in our favor. Our stop here will be much shorter than many of those around us. Perhaps the manner of loading has hastened to secure the cargo, for usually there is a much longer delay in getting the guano.

A very strange coincidence happened during our stay at the Chinchas. One day the report came that the body of a Newburyport man had been exhumed from the guano. His body had been found several feet below the surface, and at his side was a broad slab of wood, with the following inscription : —

"William Smith, Newburyport, Mass., U. S. A. Died on board Whale ship ——." The name was illegible — "Buried 1836."

Some of the details we could not make out, as the years had effaced them, but this record was sufficient to explain a mysterious disappearance. I knew the family well. For years they had watched and waited to see the boy, or to receive the word that never came. Stranger friends had laid him to rest in this isolated and deserted spot in the Pacific! They had lettered the slab at his side, knowing that at some future day it would be discovered. Commerce at last revealed it.

Wednesday, January 13, 1854. After two months, during which time we have welcomed a new year, we find we have about taken in our cargo, and are already getting into shape for a return to Callao.

The crew are busy cleaning ship, and no one can imagine the cleaning a ship needs after laying two months at anchor off the Chincha Islands. Not a part of the vessel, from the truck, to cabin and forecastle floors, escapes the fine and penetrating dust. Even closed chests, and locked boxes cannot keep it out; — inside and out they are filled and coated with the dust of guano. Everything smells of it! Bed clothes, food, deeply hidden treasures — everything has that unmistakable scent. We eat it, drink it, and sleep it; no escape, until the nuisance is left behind. We still have a few more loads to take aboard.

Our captain deserves much appreciation.

I have never sailed with a captain who so completely commands the respect and love of everybody aboard ship

SEA BIRDS IN FLIGHT

from mate to cabin-boy. Capt. Coburn is a man of very large stature, weighing fully three hundred pounds; — of commanding presence, but gentle, and kind as a woman. We all feel for him the love and respect due a father, for so he seems to us all. Notwithstanding his great weight, he can tread the ratlines as nimbly as a cat. There is a good story about him — and I believe it to be a true one — that once unaided he quelled a mutiny in which thirteen able bodied men were engaged. He certainly is a lion when aroused!

Monday, January 16, 1854. Being ready for sea, weighed anchor and ran out of the bay. Again we are headed for Callao. It was with no feeling of regret that I took my last look at those barren, guano-covered rocks. I have no love for them, and never wish to see them again.

During the whole of the stay at the islands I was filled with resentment at the cruelties practiced upon the helpless coolies, and yet being utterly powerless to lighten their sufferings I was constantly torn between pity and resentment. On the whole, the place and its memories are repugnant and loathsome! — the foul guano, with its dust, and stench, and unwholesome filth, — the gluttonous sea-monsters, the sharp cries of its songless birds, its lack of all vegetable life, and the cruelties of its taskmasters are things to be well rid of. It seemed as though nature had dumped the nuisance here to rid herself of it.

We are now well on our way to Callao. If there is no opening for a return passage to San Francisco — I have decided to remain with the ship, and return home by way of the Cape, much as I shall dislike to do so.

Chapter XXII

THE MAN OF MYSTERY

THE following incident I had decided to pass unnoted, as it was of a personal and intimate nature, but on second thought, and for certain reasons it may be wisest to relate the story. In order to do so, I must retrace my steps to the ship *Beatrice* — Capt. Rogers of Newburyport commanding — and the voyage from San Francisco to Callao; also an occurrence of nearly four years before must be recalled. The names used are fictitious.

On the day of the sailing of the *General Worth* from Newburyport, as I was about to board the brig, an old friend of my family overtook me, and after the usual "goodby" and "good luck," and "remember me when you come back with your pockets full," he drew me aside and said,

"Just a minute, Dick, I want a word with you."

We separated from the crowd at the wharf waiting to give the last Godspeed to the boys embarking for the gold-fields, and although I had known him all my life, I was a little impatient at this last minute to be detained. However, the face of my neighbor had such a serious expression, that I knew he was not holding me lightly.

"You remember my brother John?" he continued. All around us was commotion and excitement; many last words were to be spoken; baggage was being hurried aboard, and at such a time it seemed poor judgment, or rather lack of judgment to speak of family matters.

146

Somewhat impatiently I turned as though to leave him.

"Only a minute, boy — I have a message to you from father."

That was quite a definite matter, and at once I became all attention. My neighbor repeated his question.

"Do you remember John — could you recognize him if you were to see him?"

"Why, yes, I think so." Slowly out of the years came the face of a man, whom I had seen daily while I was a small lad, but who had suddenly disappeared. Whenever I had heard his name spoken later there had ever been a shaking of the head, or a "poor John," or some tone of regret to impress me with the thought that he had been surrounded by mystery.

"I am sorry to keep you now, but only a minute more," persisted my neighbor. "To understand the message father has sent to you, you must know why my brother left home. More than ten years ago he and father had a falling out — my brother rushed from the house declaring he would never return. So far he has kept his word. But we have heard from him through others who have seen him. Several times word has come that he has been recognized as a sailor on vessels sailing from ports in the Pacific. Father is old you know, and wants very much to see him. His message to him is —" and he grasped my hand as though entrusting me with something very precious, 'tell John to come home!'"

I returned the warm hand pressure, and assured him that I would bear in mind all that he had told me. He was also to say to his father that I would be on the lookout for John while on the Pacific Coast.

"One thing that may give you a clue," he added as he was leaving, "if you should be misled by his name. John has dropped the family name of Jackson" — that is not the one he used — "and is known by his middle name Smith."

I left him, and boarded the brig, at the same time promising that in some manner his message should be delivered to his brother, if I should find him.

Now the scene must be changed to the deck of the ship *Beatrice*, under the command of Capt. Rogers of Newburyport. The second mate of the vessel was a silent, reserved man, and I judged nearing the middle milestone. From my first glance this man attracted my interest; — dignified, with the far-away look to his eyes, that usually goes with the man accustomed for years to scanning the ocean horizon.

In the hours when he was off duty I tried to start a conversation to which he might respond, but his replies, while always courteous, were brief; his words were well-chosen, and his speech was the speech of the easterner, yet he never claimed that part of the country as his home. Sometimes when he was off duty, we Newburyport fellows gathered round him, and always the conversation would drift to the old home, and anecdotes of boyhood pranks would be retold, and familiar names mentioned, but the mate only listened closely, and told nothing more of his own history than that he lived in Callao with his family.

One clear evening I came upon him looking out over the rail of the ship apparently lost in thought. I said "good evening" and stopping stood beside him, — arms leaning on the rail, eyes gazing through the brief light of the tropic twilight. How could I move this man to talk to me? — this man of mystery! How could I break through the reserve with which he had walled himself about, to repeat that message from my neighbor. Had I been sure that in the second mate of the *Beatrice* I was facing John Smith Jackson, I would have given him his brother's word as he had given it to me, but as yet I was not fully convinced, although much pointed to the fact that this man was he.

I made some trivial comment on the night, the course of the ship, and the speed she was under. The mate replied civilly enough, until I ventured to ask him if he had ever sailed in the Atlantic, or visited New England. At that his manner became silent, and seemingly lost in thought he stood for a time looking out over the ocean, then hearing the strike of the bells he said,

"That's eight bells," and without more ado turned and left me.

The day came when we were nearing Callao. Again one evening I saw him standing alone as before. Again I approached him, and joining him, followed the gaze of his eyes searching the ocean. For some minutes we stood silent — neither of us speaking. Then I said,

"We are nearing port, Mr. Smith" — that was the name by which we all addressed him — "I understand you live in Callao?"

"Yes," he answered, "my family live there, and so do I when on shore."

"Does an easterner ever become accustomed to the

speech and manners of the Peruvians?" — somewhat im-
plying that I considered him from the east —

"Oh, yes, one can get accustomed to most anything."
He replied with a cynical laugh.

"By your speech," following closely, "I know you are
a native of the east — I should say New England. I find
that section of the country well represented here on the
Pacific Coast." He nodded in assent. "They come here
for various reasons. For myself, I am a gold-hunter, or —
at least I was one. At present I am a defunct gold-
hunter."

"Ah, you have not been in luck! Are you on the
return trip?"

"Not yet. I want to make another try at it. I shall
return to San Francisco from Callao."

"I think it doubtful if you find a vessel going in that
direction at this season; and also, I believe the rush to
the gold-fields of California is over."

"It's not only the pursuit of gold that draws people to
the coast," I answered. "There are many calls. There's
commerce for instance. The New England states build
many fine craft. Many good ships have been built and
have sailed from my home town of Newburyport, — not
only to the coast, but to all the ports of the world where
business of that kind is carried on. Then," after a pause,
"there are domestic troubles also that send a man out
into the world — to get as far away as possible from his
early associations. Misunderstandings arise, that easily
could be explained if an opportunity for an explanation
ever came."

We fell silent again. Mr. Smith's glance was as distant and unrecognizing as if I had not stood by his side.

Insisting upon returning to the trail that I had entered, I pursued my way.

"There was an example of such estrangement at home. In fact I was entrusted, just as I boarded the brig to sail for California, with a loving and urgent message to a wanderer — from his aged father."

The mate's expression was unchanged — he apparently listened unmoved to what I had been saying. But it seemed that there *must* be a vulnerable spot in his armor. I tried again.

"The old man's message was 'tell John I want to see him before I die! Tell him to write to me if only a word.'"

The mate stood with his hands tightly clasped. His eyes fell, and — perhaps I fancied it — the lines of his mouth tightened; but when he spoke it was with no direct reply to anything I had said.

"You are right, I have seen many ships, and many men from your part of the east. New England is a ship-building center, and you have fine captains — none better. In my time I have sailed under many of them, and ought to know what I 'm talking about. As for me — I now am a Peruvian. My home is in Callao, — at least, when it 's not on the ocean. My wife is a native of that country — my children are Peruvians. They would not understand the east, nor would the east understand them. I have left all other ties behind me. Those that were formed in a time of great trouble, are the only ones I recognize.

"Ah, eight bells. Good evening, Mr. Hale," and with

his usual abruptness the mate turned and with a slight nod went his way.

This man had neither denied nor admitted that he was the missing son. Yet, many things pointed to the fact that he was the one of whom I was in search. The name, although the same that my neighbor at home had mentioned as that his brother was known by on the Pacific, did not really prove convincing, although coinciding with what he had told me, for there were many Smiths on the seas. I did not fully recognize or recall his features, although his face seemed familiar to me, and especially his manner of talking. However, *I* felt convinced that in this man on the *Beatrice* I had discovered the brother and son of my Newburyport neighbors. But I knew that the family would never be convinced, — and that it would be all for the best. I would not have wished the aged father to know how his message had been received — *if* the son had received it.

Chapter XXIII

THE PRESS-GANG AND THE SAILOR

Monday, January 17, 1854, finds us again anchored in Callao Roads. There is no opening for a return trip to 'Frisco, so shall remain where I am, and try another journey "round the Horn." Our destination is Baltimore.

Many of the crew who shipped to the Chinchas have left us, as they engaged to go only to the islands and return. Their places have been filled by new men — among the number a second mate, cook, and steward. We are now all ready for sea.

Tuesday, January 24, 1854. On the broad Pacific, and it is much to my disappointment that I find myself on a vessel headed in the wrong direction, for I am not yet ready to face homeward, with the mission for which I started unfulfilled.

It would seem, to judge from present appearances, that the ship is under able officers, and with but two exceptions, capable men forward. The crew are certainly far above the average run of sailors. Many of them have served as officers on other vessels. They had joined in the mad rush to the coast for gold, and not having met with success in making fortunes in dust or nuggets, were now on their way home, there to ship again as officers.

There is a most unjust and wicked practice here on the Pacific Coast, and I believe it is resorted to in European

153

countries — the impressment of men as sailors. We have
two examples of this cruel custom aboard ship — I shall
speak of them later. It seems when a ship is but a short
time in port, and the captain wishes to secure men, it is
necessary for him to apply to agents. These men — at
least some of them — are merciless rascals, who fill their
orders, and secure their men in any manner in which they
can get hold of them. I was told one ship put to sea from
Callao, with a crew supposed to be composed of able
first class seamen. But on being mustered it was found
there were but two fit for duty. The others were gathered
from all kinds of professions and trades, including even
an ex-lawyer and a schoolteacher, while the rest were
laborers. The greater number were carried on to the ship
unconscious — either drunk or drugged. I cannot vouch
for the truth of the story, but I was an eye witness in the
case of the two men aboard our vessel. They were brought
to the ship unconscious — drunk or drugged! One fellow
was placed in his bunk and left there as helpless as a dead
man. When he awoke the next morning it was to find
himself well out to sea, with a month's pay taken in
advance by the "sharks" who claimed he owed it to
them for board.

Poor fellow! He awakened with a bad feeling head,
and a worse feeling heart. He found himself at sea, with
a long voyage before him, thrust into a job of which he
knew nothing, and worse yet, had no liking for. It truly
was an outrage, for which there was absolutely no remedy.
The poor chap must stay with the ship until it docked at
Baltimore. His name was Pietro Cappo, but for short we

called him Peter. He had been shipped as an able seaman, and while he suffered, perhaps our crew suffered more, for he could not tell the wheel from the windlass.

As near as we could interpret his broken English — the last that he remembered was grinding his organ in front of a sailors' boarding house. The "kind hearted" land-lord — in league with the agents no doubt — had given him money and something to drink. He remembered nothing more until he woke up and found himself out to sea. Here he was with empty pockets — with excitable gestures he proved just how empty they were — his organ gone! He tore his hands through curly black hair. His monkey — "Ah, my monka, he taka away!" — Without doubt his best and only understanding friend stolen by the rascals! He gave way to a passionate burst of weeping.

If it had not been for the indignation we felt with the agents, it would have been amusing. In fact, later Pietro did become the butt of the wags, but he accepted it all in such good spirit, that instead of suffering he really gained because he did not resent it.

While Pietro was certainly an object of pity, he also was most laughable because of his grotesqueness, and the amazement and wonder with which he gazed at every-thing connected with the brig, and her occupants. He would stare at the sails and rigging, wide eyed and cower-ing, as though he thought they were carrying him to his destruction, then turn his gaze toward the men as though they were responsible for his present plight. He would go in search of the captain and cry,

"Taka me backa! Oh, oh, taka me backa!"

But Captain Coburn, who was as much hampered and distressed to find this poor "land lubber" thrust upon him, as Pietro was distressed to be here, would reply kindly,

"I am sorry, but you 'll have to stay with the ship until she reaches port."

Whereat Pietro would tear his hair, and wring his hands, and burst into tears.

Unfortunately for Pietro, the first mate, who was not only a fine seaman, but a strict disciplinarian chose him for a member of his watch. We all were sorry for poor Peter, for the mate made no allowance for lack of experience, or lack of mental ability in his men. They all must come under one standard, or feel the effects of his rash temper. But he had selected him, and we felt the poor organ-grinder was doomed to a bitter fate. We had hoped Peter would fall to Mr. Spark's—the second mate's—watch, for he was kind hearted, of even disposition, and all the crew liked him. But Peter's luck was against him, and we all felt he was "in for it!"

One morning as I was busy below, I heard the mate's voice ringing out above. His words came faster and louder, mixed with profanity, and awful threats, and soon they were punctuated by the cries of Peter. On reaching the deck, there lay Peter — face downward, with blood streaming from his nose, while the mate stood over him with clenched fists. The noise soon brought the captain. It was the only time throughout the entire months of the voyage that I saw the big man angry, and the mate stood in great fear of him. Captain Coburn took in the trouble at a glance, and turning to the mate with eyes that withered and condemned him, said,

"You are carrying things too far, Mr. Bowers! If the men are not what they should be, do you think bruising, and abusing them will mend matters? If any more striking occurs on this vessel" — turning to the mate — "I shall have a hand in it." Ordering one of the men to assist Peter to his feet, and to cleanse his bruises, the captain left us.

I could not but feel the advantage of personality, the captain commanding others, and also in full command of himself — the mate nearly as large in stature, but possessed of a temper that completely controlled him, and often made others suffer from its effects. There were no more blows given during the trip, while the crew felt safer knowing they were protected from abuse by the captain, whom they finally grew to respect as a father.

Notwithstanding the severe reprimand the mate had received, he yet could not rid himself of the thought that ignorance on board ship was criminal, and must be punished in some manner. It never appealed to him to instruct Peter, that would have been absurd, from his standpoint. So while he did no more striking, strong language and threats followed Peter whenever the mate had occasion to give him orders, or come in touch with him. The very sight of the mate put Peter in a quiver. Yet the poor organ-grinder was ever willing to obey, but often his very eagerness got him into trouble. At the first glance of the mate he would jump, but invariably jumped in the wrong direction.

He could not steer, go aloft or splice a rope, though he could sometimes pull one, but generally he pulled the wrong one. And though very nearsighted, his favorite post was on the lookout. For here he was at peace, and free from the commands of the master he so feared. They said Peter could not see ten feet ahead, yet he was ever seeing objects miles in the distance. In a loud husky voice he would cry,

"See! See! A biga Sheep! A biga Sheep!"

But the wheelsman paid little attention to his ships, and they passed unnoticed. His defective eyes sometimes got him into trouble in the galley, mistaking it for the forecastle, especially when the cook was out, and though reproved for it, his poor eyesight often caused him to repeat the blunder. Another thing he blamed his bad sight for, was a habit he had of getting into boots that did not belong to him. But the boots generally proved much better than his own! Sometimes he got outside of his messmates meat or coffee, his eyes were so poor — if the coffee or meat was left unguarded.

Poor Peter seemed to revolve in a kind of half-circle. If he shook hands, its action described a semi-circle. If he nodded, it was the same curving motion. His course in walking lay in a curve. Perhaps his business when on land, that of "grinding" had caused it.

I describe Peter at such length for the reason that on the sea little things take prominent places, and as time passed Peter became an object of much amusement, furnishing the entire ship's company with harmless diversion, and thereby faring much better himself, for they excused some of his failings, that otherwise would have been punished.

One day as I passed the mate he called to me. Even *he* was now less severe with Peter than he had been. Occasionally a smile instead of a threat accompanied a command.

"I have just discovered what Peter is fit for, for he's certainly good for nothing else. Wait — you'll agree with me, I think."

Certainly the mate had something "up his sleeve," but he added, "He makes me so infernal nervous, I can't stand him. He's willing enough to work, but it is always in the wrong way. I tell him to let go the sheets — he's sure to get hold of the halyards — to take in slack, he's sure to ease off. Yesterday I told him to set on the spanker sheets, as the wind was light and hauling ahead, and I knew he could easily have done it, — I even pointed to the sheets and block. When I came back there he was — *sitting* on the blocks. This morning I told him to give the trunk a little scrubbing, and the first thing I knew he'd drenched the cabin, washing the chest there. He's a dangerous blunder-head — not safe to have around." But the mate at the same time he said it was laughing and added,

"Wait — I've found out what he's good for," and turned and went away with a knowing smile that showed he was not as displeased as he seemed.

Not long after I heard a commotion on deck, and hastened to see what was up. There at the weather rail stood a strange figure on the lookout for "squall."

We had an actor on board, and from him Mate Bowers had obtained a complete suit of the continental period — broad-tailed coat, high collar, vest reaching to the hips, short breeches, with knee buckles, long black stockings and low-cut shoes. A high cocked hat, and an immense pair of leather spectacles finished Peter's outfit. There the mate had stationed him — at the weather rail looking for squalls. Well, we all enjoyed the joke, and it showed also that Mate Bowers saw the ludicrous side of even a bad proposition, and had set himself to make the best of it.

We all gathered around the old continental, with Italian dialect, looking for squalls, and a great laugh went up. The captain heard the noise, and came himself to see what it was all about. He quickly retired, turning aside his face before he should utterly lose his dignity. But we knew he joined in the laughter when out of sight. When he had disappeared the mate turned to me and said,

"I guess the old man can't see much cruelty in that."

Peter stood as if on duty, taking all seriously, seemingly not aware that he was the object of the fun. Perhaps pleased at the change in his former severe master.

Our other victim of the "press-gang," soon adapted himself to the conditions under which he found himself, and became a very good sailor. At the wharf in Baltimore I lost sight of these fellows, and I do not know whether they ever returned to the Pacific Coast, or contented themselves in the east. The custom was most dastardly, and not only were the men pressed into the service of the sea the sufferers, but usually, from officers to crew they all were hampered in their duties.

CLIPPER SHIP RACER.   BUILT IN NEWBURYPORT.
1696 TONS

Chapter XXIV

THE MASSACRE AT THE STRAITS

THE return voyage "round the Horn" would not be complete if the tragic story of Harry Feely should be omitted. Harry Feely was the ship's cook, but as we came to know him aside from his duties, we found him to be an unusual man — well educated and undoubtedly of a good English family. While on the coast I had been constantly reminded of the far call the word "gold" had sounded, and of the varying conditions of men who had listened and followed its lure. Harry had heard it in his far-away English home — had traversed two oceans to answer it, and was now returning as cook on the ship *Pauline* — again over the two oceans, with but few nuggets to repay him — his lack of gold more than supplied by his wealth of experience.

He was a man of many talents, which before leaving home had been cultivated. He had a fine tenor voice. On fair calm nights he entertained us, his songs adding a charm to the hour as they floated out into the quiet reaches of the ocean. He could tell a story well, — in a manner that revealed the culture of his early training, by his speech, and by his pleasing personality. Could there have been a greater contrast to the cook of the *Beatrice?* And is it not true, that in the years of one's youth are formed the habits of mind, as well as of body that follow one into later life? Less imprint is made as time passes. And so it was with Harry. Excitement and tragedy had crowded upon him during his early years. He had been on the ill-starred English ship *Prince Albert,* wrecked in trying to work through the Straits of Magellan. Many aboard our ship knew the fact, and we hoped to get him to tell about it.

One evening Harry seemed to be in a communicative mood, and we gathered around him, all eager to listen to his account of the tragedy of the Straits.

He began in an agreeable voice, while we gave heed as he related the details of his story.

"We had entered the Straits," he began, "and were having a favorable time. Of course we had to resort to many expedients to push the ship through — towing, kedging as auxiliary to the sails — sometimes using the kedge anchor — fastening warp to objects on shore — whatever we might do to expedite matters in the treacherous and tortuous waters of the Straits. However, all seemed favorable, and we felt that in a short time more we should get out of the dangerous and crooked waters onto the broad Pacific. As I said before, all was going well, and perhaps we became over-confident. For some time a group of savages had followed us. On shore, and in their rude canoes they had trailed after the ship, seemingly friendly enough, only eager to get what they could from the passengers, and the crew on our vessel. Frequently I had thrown food, and small articles of clothing to them, more out of curiosity than from any real sympathy with them, for they were a set of brutal looking rascals as I had ever laid my eyes on.

"Suddenly the force of a current set us on a hidden bank! Nothing we could do would release the ship, — she was stuck! Fast aground! In a last attempt to float her, we were bending the hawser to a steady object ashore, every man of the crew driving himself to the limit. All were on the jump to keep the ship from laying her bones in the mud of the Straits. Orders rang out to man the windlass for a last trial. Not one, from officers to crew but was struggling to do his share to get the ship afloat! At this moment when everyone was engaged with the ship — at this moment when attention was wholly directed toward the plight of the vessel, the savages came down upon us! Swarming over the sides — great powerful brutes, — armed with knives, — bent on murder and plunder!

"Taken wholly unawares the entire company were at the mercy of the wildmen — the vessel helpless! — the crew unprepared and unsuspicious! But they fought for their lives, — those who were not cut down at once! In a moment or two the decks became slaughter shambles! I saw my chum fall as a brute thrust his reeking knife into his side, and I was powerless to go to his assistance, for at that moment a powerful savage gripped me. In the struggle with him, he got the advantage, and was just about to finish me, when another savage seized his arm before it could descend with its bloody knife. Staying his arm, he muttered a word that I could not understand, but it was enough to save my life! In a swift glance I recognized him as one to whom I had thrown bread, and other trifling gifts. The first brute loosened his mighty hold on me to fall upon and finish another victim.

"As the savage released me, I almost stumbled over the body of my chum. We had been inseparable, and he had confided to me the story of his engagement to a lovely girl in England. I bent over him, raising his head with my hands. As I did so his eyes opened, and for the instant he recognized me. With his failing strength he whispered,

"'Open my coat, — letter — to her.'

"Quickly I did as he said, found the letter, and hastily thrust it into my pocket. With a long sigh my friend breathed his last.

"The scene around me was a horrible spectacle of slaughter and plunder. So suddenly had the savages rushed down, and fallen upon the men, that they had no time to protect themselves from the deadly blows of their great, muscular assailants, each armed with a knife. But they fought for their lives with whatever lay within reach. It was a losing fight! They were entirely over-powered in numbers, by the great strength of the ruffians, and the unexpectedness of the attack.

"The lives of two others had been spared, and for similar acts to my own — small gifts of food or other trifles. We three fellows were forced over the side of the ship, and by unmistakable threatening gestures, told to get on our way. This we did as quickly as possible, swimming ashore, and when reaching there, hiding as best we could. Thus we laid our course over a barren and unknown coast.

"For three days we followed the shore, eating bits of seaweed, little fish, or whatever the bleak beach afforded. On the morning of the fourth we captured a duck, and raw as it was, it proved the sweetest morsel I had ever tasted.

"The morning of the fifth day brought us to a small settlement near the eastern entrance of the Straits. Fortunately we were rescued by a vessel headed for England.

"On arriving in England my first duty was to find the sweetheart of my chum, and give her his last message. She opened the letter, and read its contents. I had already prepared her as well as I could, by telling her that her lover was dead, yet omitting many of the painful details. Naturally it proved a great blow to her. From the first moment I saw her beauty, and realized her goodness, and felt her grief over the death of her lover, I loved her. And so I waited my time — until her loss should grow less heavy, and her sorrow less keen.

"The news of the discovery of gold in California reached England. I had almost despaired of ever winning her, and so decided to try my luck in the gold-fields. Just before I sailed, I learned that she had grown to care. And," he added looking at his listeners as though hoping for their approval, "I am now on my way home to make her my wife."

Harry's last sentence came as a happy climax to a tragic tale. After returning from the scene of the massacre — for it was some moments before we could warm to this last bit of romance — we congratulated him on the happy ending.

When Harry said good-by in Baltimore he gave me this address, and requested me to write to him: Harry Feely, Pennyfield, Poplar, London, Eng.

Among our crew the ablest of the forecastle, if not of the entire ship was Charles Bunker of Nantucket. He had strayed from duty in listening to the call of the siren, and capable officer as he had ever before proved, was now returning from the gold-fields to New Bedford, where he hoped to take a mate's position on an outward bound whaler, from there to the Pacific whaling grounds.

He was one of the best read and informed sailors I had ever met. He might have been about thirty years of age, and he had accumulated a fund of information that should have fitted him for an instructor. He was not only a thorough navigator, but he was also a good astronomer — familiar with the heavens and their peoples, the stars and the planets, as I was with my landmarks, and the faces of my friends. Many a clear night I have gazed at the stars and he has made me acquainted with the inhabitants of the distant skies. Charles Bunker left the ship at Baltimore proceeding without delay to New Bedford.

Sunday, February 5th. We have two sick sailors aboard, but they were not thought to be in a serious condition, until last evening when the disease was pronounced yellow fever. One sick man seems to be much better, while I fear the other is worse — little hope of his recovery.

Monday, February 6th. One of the yellow fever patients died today. We knew little about him. His name was John Fischer, and to judge from his speech, he was a

German. All his shipmates liked him, and said he was a capable seaman. During his sickness he showed much courage, even taking his condition as a matter to joke about — telling those around him the pranks he would play upon them when he got about again.

A burial at sea is depressing, and brings great gloom to the ship. The body of John Fischer was wrapped in his hammock, the folds secured tightly and sewed together around him, the feet heavily weighted. A plank holding the body was placed on the gangway rail, the inner end, near the head, was held by two sailors. Top sails abacked, the vessel stood almost motionless. Passengers and crew gathered around, heads uncovered, silently listening to the last rites of a sailor buried at sea. Captain Coburn read the prayer, and repeated the service. Then, at a motion of his hand, the two seamen raised the end of the board. Slowly the form moved down the incline and fell into the ocean. A splash! An eddy of bubbles and foam! The waters united, and John had disappeared forever.

Each one present felt a grip of sorrow, and regretted the need that demanded a prompt burial in the deep. Our community was so small, there was so little diversion except what each one contributed, that with the splash of the wave, our spirits seemed to follow the weight of the lead that drew poor John to his last home.

No one knew him. No one could tell of his fate to waiting relatives. His life was a blank to us, and seemed symbolic of the great mystery into which he sank.

Everything in readiness, the ship filled away again on her course. As I stood watching the surface of the sea flowing so placidly above the spot where John's body had disappeared, these lines came to my mind,

"Nothing of him that doth fade,
But doth suffer a sea-change
Into something rich and strange."

Chapter XXV

ON THE HOME STRETCH

FEBRUARY 15th. Lat. 40° 58' south, Lon. 86° 42' west. We are again from studding sails to close reefs — changing winds and changing sails!

Our yellow fever suspect quickly recovered after John Fischer's death, and almost immediately he reported for duty. He also promptly appeared at the galley for rations. Whatever the cause, he at present appears in good health, and is doing able seaman's work.

February 26th. Passed Diego Ramirez about fifteen miles distant — barren, desolate rocks, named in honor of the great discoverer. A cold and bleak monument to one who had the courage to brave the untried seas. Yet could there be a more fitting pile reared to the memory of one who dared the uncharted ocean and blazed the first trail that others might follow? Rocks carved by the creative hand, lashed by the storms and waves of the centuries, to stand a monument to their discoverer so long as the solid earth remains!

We are now in Cape waters. Our ship has been thoroughly overhauled, and is in fine condition to meet the rigours of the Cape. The old sails have been unbent and stored below, and new ones bent in their places. Rigging has been reset, and everything is in fine ship order. At noon today sighted, and passed the Cape. At 2 P. M. sank it in the distance.

February 27th. Made and passed Staten Land. The same snow-bound, ice-clad rock we so gladly bade adieu more than four years ago. The weather was clear, and with a glass the seals, penguins and sea-fowl could be distinguished sporting along its shores. However, the skies cleared but for a time. They again shut down upon us, and squalls of sleet and snow are driving the ship, and pelting the men. Knowing what to expect we were ready for it. Yet cold rations, and wet and cold clothing for days begin to be unendurable. A little more head today and our ship would have barked an iceberg. A great fellow, frowning out of the fog, it lay in our path. The vessel changed her course just in time. It was my first glimpse of an iceberg. The air is still cold and smells of ice. Today marks our most southern limit. Our bow soon will be pointing homeward, to be freed from the region of our foes!

Sunday, March 19th. Today crossed the tropic of Capricon. We have not yet been favored by the southeast trades. The winds are varying, at times too strong, and again not enough breeze to fill the sails, or even to keep them from slatting, by motion of the swell or roll of the vessel.

Thursday, March 23d. This is our first day of southeast trades, and though tardy they are welcome, for they are pushing us on in the right direction.

Wednesday, 29th. Our trades have forsaken us. We

were favoured with them for a week, but now they have
left us to be the sport of squalls, bafflings or calms. Several vessels steering to the south have passed us. Among
the number one English ship came within hailing distance.

April 4th. Crossed the Equator this morning in Lon.
40°, and by noon observation we were 24 miles north
of it. The northeast trades are favoring us. We ran into
them in Lat. 1° 23' south, and though light they are
pushing us along as well as we can expect. All light
sails are set to catch all the trades can give.

Friday, April 7th. Fine weather with moderate trades
wafting us toward home. This evening saw the North
Star rise above the horizon in Lat. 3° north. We welcomed it as an old friend. Everything now is beautiful,
the breeze favouring, the sea smooth. In fact I am feeling
quite kindly toward old father Neptune, for today his
realm is more lovely than the land. No dust, no dirt, he
wears an irresistable beauty that cannot fail to charm.

No aloft duty today. In fact but little duty at all. The
watch below are sleeping. The watch on duty, reading,
writing or playing games. The only working man is at the
wheel, and steering is light. An ideal life, — this life in the
tropics with us today !

In this guise old Neptune lures the unwary into his
service, and when once in his grasp they are his forever.
A sailor on shore soon sighs for his ocean home and fare.
Thus old Neptune peoples his ships with his captives.

Large schools of flying fish dart over the wave about us.

They often take wing to avoid their dread foe the dolphin, but usually the dolphin's fins are fleeter than the tiny wings.

April 14th. The trades still favour us. The breeze though fair is light, and our progress not very swift. It is how-ever, good working weather for the watch on duty — put-ting on new ratlines, and tarring down rigging. Lat. 18° 11′ north, Lon. 59° 01′ west.

Saturday, 15th. Trades still moderate. By observation find we are 1270 miles southeast, half south, from Cape Henry, one of the headlands of the Chesapeak. This morning sailed through large fields of floating seaweed.

Chapter XXVI

GOLD AT THE END OF THE RAINBOW

Monday, April 17th. Today crossed the tropic of Cancer in Lon. 65° 46', which brings us again into the temperate zone. We are in northern waters, and now I realize that we are really on the home stretch. After an absence of nearly five years I am facing home. Mingled emotions stir me! What changes would the course of the years disclose? What had this bearded man, myself, lined and bronzed by exposure, in common with the stripling who had gone in quest of the "pot of gold at the foot of the rainbow" years before? If the wear of time had so altered me, how had it changed those left behind? It was with a feeling of dread that I pictured the first greetings. Would we meet almost as strangers? Would my mother and father warm to this rugged man, as they had to the vanished boy?

The gold that I sought to wrest from mines in the Eldorado, I had failed to discover, and viewed from that angle, the months of searching had been a complete fiasco. Yet, while I should have liked to return with well-filled pockets, to thus prove the wisdom of the venture, which had been discouraged at the start by those more cautious, — I could still say that it had all been a most valuable experience.

Wednesday, April 19th. Light, baffling winds for the

greater part of the day. In the early morning and late at night heavy rain squalls, accompanied by thunder and lightning. No observation today.

Thursday, April 20th. Calm in the morning. Later a breeze sprang up from N. E. which obliged us to tack ship. We are now fairly out of the trades with winds varying from N. E. to N. W., — Lat. 27° 52′ N., Lon. 67° 47′ W.

Friday, 21st. Light wind from the N. N. W. A dull monotonous sea-day, with only the thought that we are nearing home to break the tediousness of watching the bowsprit point seaward, to escape a light wind coming from the direction in which we wish to lay our course. Today passed a barque steering southwest. At noon find we have sailed and drifted until reaching Lat. 28° 09′ N., Lon. 68° 44′. Any kind of a change but a head storm would be welcome. These calms are hard to endure, when passengers and crew are eager to reach port.

Saturday, 22nd. Began with the same light wind that dwindled at times to a calm, which fortunately soon changed to the N. N. E. However, though light, the change was acceptable, for now we are headed in the right direction. At three o'clock in the afternoon we were aroused from our lethargy by sighting a mysterious craft making tracks in our direction. We watched her with considerable curiosity. She came on like a race-horse, and word went from lip to lip,

"What do you make of her?" "Is she a pirate?"
"She 's sure on our track!"

For a few minutes it seemed as though we might be in
for some trouble, for she certainly was bound on a mission of some sort and her bowsprit was headed directly
toward us. However, we were not the objective, for she
passed us without speaking — racing on, seeming more
eager to show us her taffrail than bow, which she quickly
did, for she was a "fleet-footer," just in good ballast trim
to *give* us a "goodby," even if she was not civil enough to
say it. The mystery-ship passed as easily as though we
had been an old lumber droger lying at anchor.

Sunday, April 23d. The light N. N. E. breeze still
favouring, we are slowly gaining in the run northward.
This may be our last Sunday at sea — at least, we all hope
so. Land so near inspires everyone to come into port
looking his best. We shall try to make a brave showing.
Our ship has been overhauled and painted, while at
present the crew are blacking their boots, and bringing to
light their heavy blue pilots, and flannels. Jack-tar is
proud as a peacock when ashore, but often suffers from
overstepping his bounds on land, where he is free from
the strict discipline under which he is ever ruled while at
sea.

At noon passed an hermaphrodite brig; at 3 o'clock a
fore-and-after steering north; at 6 o'clock P. M. a ship
heading south. At noon our Latitude was 28° 41', north,
Lon. 70° 44'. By observation of the north star at evening
— Lat. 28° 40'.

Monday, April 24th. Nearly a dead calm—hardly wind
enough to give us steering way. During the day a squall
accompanied with rain, swept down upon us without
warning, and without warning left us as suddenly as it
came; but it changed our light winds coming from no-
where in particular, to a fine southwest breeze. There is
now some motion to the ship, and the atmosphere is clear
and bracing. However, later we were doomed to disappointment again, for it dwindled into almost a calm,
and we are now drifting with nearly idle sails. It was
unfortunate the squall did not leave us the strong and
lasting wind we had hoped for. Even our captain is growing impatient — to judge by his expression, and the unmistakable way in which he avoids questions, at times
muttering indistinctly to himself. Were our next port
not home we might bear this delay with a better spirit.
The day is leaving us a strong northeast wind, accompanied by a heavy head sea. Lat. 30° 21', Lon. 70° 33'.

Thursday, April 27th. There was so little of interest to
note in the past two days,—nothing but calms and
bafflings, that I passed them by without the waste of ink
and paper.

Today all is bustle and activity. We have set the sails
to catch the strong easterly breeze. This soon hauled to
the south southwest, but did not lessen our speed. We
are now making good time, and traveling along in fine
style. The Gulf Stream is in our wake, and though land
is not yet in sight, sometimes we imagine we can smell
it. Soon after midnight made Ocracock Light, bearing

west northwest, about ten miles distant. On sounding, found 11 fathoms of water. Wore ship and stood to the southeast. Soon after laid our course to the southeast, and at noon came up to northwest. Lat. 35° 50′ north, Lon. 74° 40′ west. Distance from Cape Henry 88 miles northwest, one quarter north.

Friday, April 28th. The same southwest wind has been steadily pushing us shoreward. All eyes are eagerly strained to catch the first glimpse of land. At 6 o'clock P. M. heard the welcome and joyous cry "Land-ho." This without doubt is our last day at sea. Everything is favouring at present. The wind though light is fair, and the land sighted in the distance rolls out like low, blue-gray clouds. Fearing we might be making the land too quickly, the captain, at 7.30 o'clock gave orders to shorten sail, which was none too soon, for Cape Henry light flashed into sight, and we are following its rays into the old bay waters.

The decks are crowded, and almost as eagerly as we watched for the land through the Golden Gates, do we watch for the long-looked-for land ahead — the land of home.

Everyone is on deck — there are no sleepers or watch below. We gladly turn our backs to old ocean, for the present at least, and bid it farewell without regret. A stronger attraction than old ocean can offer lies ahead.

Soon we heard the cry, "Ship Ahoy." It was the pilot off the Cape. He boarded us, and laid our course to the anchoring ground.

To the deep-sea wanderer there is a charm in the pilot's call. He brings the first greetings from the shore, while one feels safe under his guidance, as he picks his way through the channels of the bay. The pilot is the first to break the dull monotony of sea life, and to the traveler he brings a greeting from the shore. As opportunity presents, each one secretly — the rules of the ship do not permit it — steals to him, and asks him a thousand questions of matters ashore. He not only is a most welcome guest, but he is in highest command, and all are subject to his orders. We were soon on the safe side of the Cape, where we dropped anchor for the night.

At four the next morning got under way for Hampton Roads, and reaching there again dropped anchor, this time near the Rip Raps, after a passage of 93 days from Callao. Here we passed Saturday and Sunday, and on Monday, May 1st, got under way for Baltimore, arriving there on the 3d, with everything and everybody in fine condition.

Captain Coburn was not to see the last of us without giving us a rousing good send-off, for he is a generous and noble, and withal a kindly man. On our way up he purchased several barrels of oysters, and had the cook serve them in every conceivable manner. They quickly disappeared, and on reaching the city not a bivalve remained of the load blocking the ship's waist a few hours before. With this feast our voyage ended. The final partings, no matter how great the trials shipmates have shared, are always sad. They become welded as a family, and their very adversities draw them closer. So with the company on the *Pauline;* we had shared the dangers and troubles of the voyage, and with the last handclasps we parted, each going in his own way, most of us destined never to meet again.

After a brief visit in Baltimore, and Philadelphia, I hastened on to New York, where I met my brilliant brother Enoch, then one of the editors of the *Journal of Commerce.* He greeted me first of the family, and as I feared, he did not know me until I had spoken to him. He had changed very little, for older than I, he had always seemed from childhood much my senior. Together we started on the last lap of the journey to Newburyport. There, though I found the family circle unbroken, my fears were well grounded. Time *had* touched each member, but in most cases with light fingers. With me he had worked more heavily — bronzing and bearding and broadening the smooth-faced lad, until it was hard to pick out any likeness to the boy who had left for the gold-fields. Thus the journey of over four and a half years ended on May 9, 1854, with "all well."

Only one passing through a similar experience can appreciate what the meeting with my parents meant to me, and so I shall not attempt to describe it. As word was noised abroad that the wanderer had returned, old time friends crowded in to welcome me. And while the subject of the illusive gold was always touched upon, yet the real interest centered in the vast and untraveled countries in which my years of absence had been passed — the lay of the land — the types of soil — the wonders of the giant trees — the likelihood of the primitive hamlets of the

Pacific Coast ever growing to be important cities — the
call of commerce to their ports — the minerals — the process
of development in which as a pioneer I had taken a part,
and countless other questions to which I could give intelligent replies, until at last I realized that my experiences
had been as valuable to me as the bag of gold I had come
home without. The gold might easily vanish, but that
which I had gained in pursuing the "pot of gold at the
end of the rainbow" could never be taken away.

IN RETROSPECT

Through modern lenses looking back to the days of fifty years ago, the manners, customs and usages of that time are obsolete. Where now could one find the cradle or rocker, the toin or riffle box, but within the walls of a museum — curiosities, marking an era that is past.

The records within these pages are milestones along the highway of memory. The author reads the symbols, and knows the direction in which they point, but he little understands the youth who traveled that highway. The youth surely would never have recognized him, and he scarcely recognizes the youth.

As I recall the miners of fifty years ago, I see them vigorous with youth and energy, ever firm in the belief that their Eldorado lies just ahead of them, the courage, ambition and hope natural to the young, driving them onward. If gold is not at hand, then they will find it at the top of the mountain, if not there, then in the river-bed at the mountain's foot, — with good cheer "pulling up stakes" to plant them again in more favorable places.

Since the day the author started upon the voyage of one hundred and fifty-nine days to reach the gold-fields of California, the continent has been spanned by steam, and the letter that then one must wait months to receive, is now but the same number of days in transit. The little hamlets have become great business centers; the abandoned, unpaying "diggings" have become mines of wealth and enterprise, and bustling cities prosper where the old-

181

time miner staked his claim, or built his rude cabin. But the early visitors, with their crude implements, their simple methods, and their primitive manners of traveling were, after all, the pioneers to open a vast and unexplored territory.

NOTES. On his last visit to San Francisco my father was walking through the old burial ground. At the time, the bodies of the victims of the plague were being removed to the new cemetery out near the mission. He discovered a stone that bore the name, "James Brown, Newburyport, Mass." He knew Mr. Brown's family intimately, as they had been near neighbors. Mr. Brown had been drowned shortly after reaching California, and the stone had been sent from home.

Out of respect to the family, and with the natural interest he felt in a townsman, my father interested others, and together they opened the grave, and placed the body in the new ground, leaving the lot in the order that he thought the family would desire. Within the grave he discovered two caskets — one resting on the other. On opening them, the upper one was found to contain the body of Mr. Brown, while that in the under coffin was covered with a sheet, and everything indicated an accidental death. My father believed the unknown man to have been Captain Moody of Newburyport, who was accidentally killed on his vessel at about that time. Both were conveyed to the new ground and placed as he had found them.

Note 2. After reaching home my father sought the family who had entrusted him with the message to the missing son, whom he felt convinced he had discovered on the ship *Beatrice*. But they had left the city and he could find no trace of them.

Note 3. The body of Captain Coburn's brother, who had died of yellow fever at Callao, had been enclosed in a metalic coffin and brought home buried in the guano. At Baltimore it was transferred to Dresden, Me.

Note 4. Several years after returning from the Pacific Coast my father was in Red Bank, N. J. One evening he was in a company of people who asked him to relate some of his experiences in the gold-fields. He then told of his meeting with Walter Buck. One of the number present seemed much interested, and questioned him regarding the appearance of the young bandit — the color of his eyes and hair, his stature, et cetera. My father said that he resembled the questioner, and asked if he knew Walter. The reply was that he had known him well, — as a neighbor. However, it proved that the questioner was Walter's brother.